Communication in an Expanding Organization

by the same author

The manager and the organization
Science and technology in Europe (Penguin Books)

ERIC MOONMAN

Communication in an Expanding Organization

A CASE STUDY IN ACTION RESEARCH

TAVISTOCK PUBLICATIONS
London · New York · Sydney · Toronto · Wellington

First published in 1970 by
Tavistock Publications Limited
11 New Fetter Lane, London EC4
Printed in Great Britain
in 11 pt Baskerville 2 pt leaded
by Butler & Tanner Ltd
Frome and London
© Eric Moonman 1970

SBN 422 73080 7

Distributed in the United States of America
by Barnes & Noble Inc.

Contents

	Acknowledgements	*page* vii
1	Introduction	1
2	Background to the study	13
3	Initial inquiries and report	19
4	First study in Mills F and G	25
5	Investigation at head office	42
6	Follow-up in Mills F and G	69
7	A further study in communication – Mill H	92
8	Research into action: management–staff panels	111
9	Conclusions and recommendations	127
	Appendices	143
	References	172
	General reading	174
	Index	177

For NATASHA and DANIEL

Acknowledgements

My thanks are due to my research colleagues at the University of Manchester Institute of Science and Technology for their cooperation and, in particular, I owe a debt of gratitude to Dr Arthur Roberts, Reader in Management Sciences, for his help and encouragement – a most necessary outside support to me, in view of the demands an action-research project makes on the research team leader.

The need to preserve the anonymity of the Group of companies investigated prevents me from identifying by name the staff of all levels who gave me so much help – among them the Director of Personnel and mill managers and operatives. I hope that this volume may be regarded in some measure as a repayment of my debt.

I am grateful to the British Institute of Management for allowing me to reproduce a document in the text. Thanks are also due to R. S. Stokes and T. Blount.

Finally, I alone know the enormous contribution made by my wife Jane, who offered me intellectual stimulus and relevant criticism, and always with good humour. I am indeed grateful.

E. M.

I

Introduction

THE TEXTILE INDUSTRY

Many changes have taken place in the industrial complexion of the north of England. Government encouragement has introduced newer industries, ranging from motor-car manufacture to wholly science-based operations, into old, declining areas. Yet textiles and related trades continue at the heart of Lancashire and Yorkshire because of their traditions and the many families who have and will continue to have associations with the industry. It is likely that there will always be an important role for a British textile industry if its leaders recognize the changes that must be made as a result of modern technology, management, and marketing.

One aspect of the current dilemma facing the industry is the fragmentation of many processes and operations carried on in hundreds of mills and companies. The case for greater rationalization of resources needs little emphasis now; for several years it has been understood and acted upon by leading companies throughout the country. Justification for larger units of operation is made on financial, technical, and structural grounds.

This book describes a case study of employee responses within a rapidly expanding Group of companies in the textile trade. The particular rate of expansion, both of individual mills and of the larger concentrations, makes it difficult to judge accurately all the circumstances of 'change'. The social research worker cannot hold still or satisfactorily isolate the elements of

I

individual behaviour, social environment, and organizational pressure, in such a dynamic setting. Few professionals can: the doctor, for instance, cannot stop the deterioration of a patient's condition during the course of his analysis. This is achieved later and reflects available knowledge of the subject, and the doctor's own judgement and understanding of what is wrong.

The Group of companies here under investigation is well known as a large-scale manufacturer of textiles. It will be referred to throughout this volume as the Wearwell Group. The research in which I was engaged arose out of a series of meetings and private discussions which took place in 1964 between the assistant managing director of the Group and a leading member of the Department of Management Sciences in the University of Manchester. Three research workers, one of whom left the team after a few months, began their preliminary inquiries in January 1965. The final stage of the project was completed in the late summer of 1966. I had been appointed Senior Research Fellow in the Department of Management Sciences some seventeen months earlier to coordinate the work of the research team, to organize and maintain a formal basis of communication between the Group of companies and the university, which had not existed hitherto, and, finally, to investigate and solve some of the problems of this expanding Group of companies committed to rapid organizational and technological change.

ACTION RESEARCH

The method and technique of inquiry were entirely mine. I felt it necessary to involve myself (and the research team in one particular experiment) in the organization in a way that would go beyond the production of a statement of what was happening, by, for instance, working, where appropriate, with company staff in solving some of their difficulties. Such a surrender of objectivity is, I suggest, inevitable if the dynamics of the social system are to be studied. The technique I selected, after careful consideration of the Group, its size, and its leaders, and of the aims and objectives given to me as leader of the project, was that of action research, which would give flexibility of inquiry and greater scope in handling the study bearing in mind the fairly modest research resources.

Action research is not simply a problem-solving exercise: its purpose is also creative. Kurt Lewin, one of the pioneers of the process, said (1946): 'Research which produces nothing but books will not suffice', and he underlined the dynamic nature of action research by describing it as 'research leading to social action'.

The precise benefits to be derived from action research are sometimes difficult to forecast, though they can almost always be discerned in behaviour following effective research. For instance, at a meeting of the British Institute of Management, a senior executive once said, of certain research undertaken in his plant, that no conscious use had been made of its results, but that there had been such intangible benefits as a greater sensitivity on the part of management.[1]

Thus, while the present report does contain proposals for specific action, it may be that its more important effect will be to awaken in the management to whom it is addressed a more critical and exact awareness of the problems of communication.

Although the management of Wearwell Group Ltd appeared in general to be satisfied with the Group's current aggressive expansionist policy, and although several individual members thought that the efficiency of the present communication procedure was good, they nevertheless felt that a system of communication that was adequate for the operational task at a given point in time could (and was beginning to) be less effective as the Group expanded further. It was chiefly with this in mind that, after preliminary interviews with senior executives of the Wearwell Group, I outlined the following as the aims of my inquiry:

(a) To attempt to identify the process of communication as a

[1] See report in *The Manager*, November 1965.

wholly organizational thing. In other words, to assess the attitudes of the manager along with those of his subordinate staff in each of three mills, and to follow this by a deepening of the research so as to include the employees in order to discover the effects of top organizational behaviour upon communication, performance, and labour relations. Comparisons in organizational behaviour (between the mills and headquarters) would also be made.

(b) To assess the best means and mechanism for strengthening Group communication, to establish systems involving actual programmes of personnel and management development in conjunction with the Wearwell Group Personnel Department, and to attempt to determine the most suitable system within the context of a continually expanding company.

Communication as a concept within industry has been elaborately defined by psychologists, sociologists, and structural technicians. Each specialist brings to the subject his own training, skills, and range of experience, but unfortunately there are few occasions when the specialists within the separate fields of inquiry utilize the knowledge or the approaches of the others. Yet it would seem reasonable to suppose that a real understanding of the communication process and of any practical way of overcoming the barriers to communication must produce an approach able to synthesize the three disciplines. I shall now explain what they represent.

It is not my intention nor is it my brief to detail the study of psychology; it is sufficient to say that it is the study of human behaviour based upon scientific method and that it has already made a significant contribution to industry in the fields of selection, appraisal, attitude surveys, and communication generally. I want to examine the last-mentioned application of psychology in industry since it has most markedly affected the patterns of authority.

Communication between one individual and another is a constant and continuous process. It is a means of interaction.

This is brought about when one individual is in contact with another, or when one group is associated with another. The behaviour of A in making or maintaining contact with B evokes a response from B; both A's action and B's response to it will affect A; similarly, B's response and the subsequent reaction of A make a difference to B. The interaction described may be considered to be a more complex arrangement than the simple direction of a message through the autocratic process whereby the listener is not encouraged to discriminate or to offer any comment to the speaker. It also demands more of the manager through his efforts to understand the individual differences that exist within the work group. No two men will respond to a message in the same way and it is here that the manager, by attempting to understand the individual differences, can improve the effectiveness of his communications. To 'understand' requires a consideration of the main forces that have shaped or moulded the individual: his background, experience, and education. These are just some of the things that affect the individual's personality and that have, to some extent, to be taken into account when a message is to be transmitted.

The importance of understanding the individual personality and the impact it may have upon the work group is now a commonly recognized generalization resulting from modern industrial psychological research which postulates that modern management requires new skills in leadership. Professor Robert Tannenbaum, in his basic thesis, stresses that the successful leader is one who is keenly aware of those forces motivating his behaviour at any given time. He understands himself, other individuals, and the group with which he is dealing (Tannenbaum & Schmidt, 1958).

The successful leader is one who is able to behave appropriately in the light of the needs of the group: if controlling is required, he will control; if participative leadership is more appropriate, he will encourage his subordinates to exercise initiative.

The study of sociology is equally necessary for our understanding of what holds a work group together and what gives it satisfaction. The concept of authority has undergone a considerable change since the last century when it was possible both in industry and outside to ignore the social motives of the individual, when it was possible to control a work group with little thought for its needs and aspirations. The pace of social change today requires us to give attention to the influences that have brought about what is, in some respects, a new social environment. It arises mainly from the improvement and extension of educational facilities as well as from economic advance for a great number of people in this country. The significance of education as an influence on social attitudes cannot be measured in quantitative terms alone; indeed, one of the most striking of its results is the change of emphasis in the teacher–student relationship. The formal atmosphere, the autocratic role that the teacher had assumed historically, have now, in some respects, given way to informality, to a more democratic leadership, where discussion is encouraged and experiences are shared. Similarly, the economic improvements since the 1920s and 1930s accord the individual a greater range of choice which has the ultimate effect of giving him more power, both as a consumer and as a worker.

Professor W. J. H. Sprott (1958) has described the behaviour of men and women in a series of associations, providing an invaluable guide to our study:

> We must think of groups as dynamic entities, and not as mere collections of people, haphazardly thrown together. Of course the urgency of their collective purposiveness will vary from situation to situation.

Thus the productivity unity of a work group in a factory may lie dormant for a considerable period of time and then suddenly it will be aroused and will make itself felt. In other words, the work group may for generations obediently accept the command structure – 'the manager' or 'the boss' – and then at some point of crisis it begins to act as a single entity in resisting authority. Thus it has found the occasion for a group purpose. It will be apparent to the manager how important it is for him to be aware of the social forces that exist within industry. It is not enough that the formal structure of an organization should be carefully defined; it is also necessary that the operation of the less tangible social forces should be discerned. The significance of the primary and secondary groups, described by Sprott, needs to be properly understood in any organization but particularly in one expanding rapidly, like the Wearwell Group, as we shall see later.

A great deal has been written about group dynamics in industry, yet management, in large numbers of companies, has ignored the evidence of extensive research and experience. As Douglas McGregor (1960) said:

> Every manager quite naturally considers himself his own social scientist ... The social scientist's knowledge often appears to him to be theoretical and unrelated to the realities with which he must deal.

McGregor gives a further reason for management's failure to make effective use of current social science knowledge. He says it results from a misconception of the nature of control in the field of human behaviour. It would seem that McGregor, the late Professor of Management at Massachusetts Institute of Technology, was advising the social research worker to familiarize himself with the people as well as with the technical process of the company he is studying. If the research worker succeeds at this elementary level, then his subsequent task of explaining to management the importance and effectiveness of systematic method in the human sciences will be that much easier.

Action research fulfils these requirements: it enables the research worker not only to give a detailed analysis of the company with which he is concerned, but to offer a framework in which a practical solution may be implemented, which he may assess. Some managers will be suspicious of or will resist some aspects of the researcher's task. In some respects, considerable sensitivity and understanding on the part of the researcher are called for, and he must be prepared to modify the assumptions he makes about management and the industrial environment in the light of what transpires during the research. This particular operational problem is described by Rice (1958) in his study of an Indian textile mill:

> ... we found it difficult to work together because so many of the concepts and assumptions upon which my questions and suggestions were based were implicit rather than explicit. When I tried to make them explicit I found their formulation in coherent and unambiguous terms both difficult and time-consuming. Some, which I had intuitively accepted as obvious and self-explanatory, needed considerable explanation. Others, which I thought complex and involved, were intuitively accepted by the managers as simple and straightforward.

I now come to the question of organization structure and the studies that have been made which justify a clearly defined structure as a basis for maintaining a good communication flow.

While there must be some hesitation about generalizing on the structure of different organizations and different industries, we have sufficient evidence to be able to recognize certain common patterns of formal and informal organization that exist within every company, hospital, college, or institution. The aims of the body will differ according to the policy-making group, from the provision of a service (as in the case of a hospital board) to the maximization of profits. But the structure, the pattern of authority, and the range of anticipated responsibilities may be the same.

The differences that arise between the formal and the informal structure need careful consideration (Mayo, 1933; Roethlisberger & Dickson, 1939; Homans, 1950). In any one organization there are a number of informal structures but only one formal. The latter is established by the policy-making body and extended or modified by those managers or specialists who are designated to do so. The informal group structure is the term used to indicate the sub-system, which may be a reaction against the formal structure; it is less tangible and more difficult to assess. The informal structure is created by employees in several ways. A common problem may have arisen in a department, which causes employees of different grades, skills, or functions to talk about and around the issue. No action may result from such discussion but clearly a communication system now functions which may help or hinder the manager's task. Again, the informal structure operates when workmen of a particular skill or trade meet from time to time by virtue of their occupational group, yet they may not work alongside each other or even within the same department.

An informal structure may also arise from the common interests or affiliations of the employees. Irrespective of the actual contact of employees during the working day, if, for instance, they attend the same political club, actively participate in the works welfare facilities, or are members of the same church, a further link in informal communication outside working hours is made which can be brought back into the firm.

Organizational or technological change may demand a new approach to the flow of information within a company. It is this proposal that this study will attempt to illustrate. Two other studies are relevant here. During an investigation carried out by Burns and Stalker (1961) of Edinburgh University, the researchers persuaded the members of the top management of a number of firms to keep a record, on simple diary schedules, of how they spent their working time every day for three or more weeks. The results included the amount of time spent by each manager, and the management staff of each firm, in conversation, in writing, in reading memoranda and letters, in dealing with routine records, and so forth. It became quite clear that the more strongly a firm was committed to a changing situation – in design, process, market, or size – the greater was the proportion of time spent by managers in conversation. The range was from 80 per cent for a firm heavily involved in developments based on recent technical advances in electronic control systems, to 42 per cent for a branch factory producing one or two standard items of equipment with changes in volume. Design and method were dealt with and planned for elsewhere. The amount of time devoted to report-writing was also appreciably high.

The evidence points to a principal organizational difference between firms in stable and firms in changing situations. In the first kind, the individual manager normally has a clearly designed function, and the manner and direction in which communication is made are also laid down from above. But in a firm in which changes of market, design, or manufacturing methods are taking place all the time, there is no possibility of one man's knowing all the kinds and sources of information that he would need to know to do his job successfully.

A study in a textile manufacturing company takes this concept somewhat further. The dynamics of a changing technology, it is concluded, demand a cooperative frame of reference for the manager:

> Because of the broad sweep of the operation and the relative lack of existing linkages, 'leadership' in the sense of establishing goals, setting limits, and actuating wider loyalties becomes very necessary indeed (Fensham & Hooper, 1964).

From these and other studies it seems highly credible that the authority flowing to persons by virtue of the place they occupy in the chain of command is not a barometer of the real power and control within a company or department.

Put briefly, this research project attempts to use these three areas of inquiry – psychology, sociology, and organizational theory – in the study of communication within an expanding company. This interaction of social and technical change was used by Trist and Bamforth in 1951 in an investigation of the longwall method of coal-getting, and by Rice in the study referred to earlier, with considerable effect. I was interested not only in what was said by various levels of staff in the Group of companies but also in how their attitudes were formed.

It is now necessary to define 'communication' more exactly. I have elsewhere described the process of communication in the following terms:

The passing on of feelings and ideas by an individual or group to another individual or group, and, where necessary, the evoking of a discriminating response. This means that the message must be fully understood in all its implications and, where appropriate, answered by the receiver. If the process is executed in this way, creative participation will be stimulated (Moonman, 1961).

The important point is that communication in the stricter sense may, and in an industrial context often should, consist of more than the basic ingredient of passing on information. Feedback is required but is difficult to foster effectively: it is more especially when we require a return flow of information that we say the interaction of human or group behaviour becomes 'difficult' or 'complicated'.

Thus, to achieve communication in its fullness demands the discharge of responsibilities by both the transmitter and the recipient of a message. But it is the transmitter, or, in our case, the manager, who bears the heavier responsibility, since he is in the controlling position and able, at least to some extent, to plan and arrange the variables by, for instance, modifying the atmosphere of a department, or making structural alterations. In short, he is the leader.

Style can make or mar communication as a creative, two-way process. Gross (1964) cites the following two methods of expressing the same message:

England expects every man to do his duty.

England anticipates that as regards the present emergency personnel will face up to the issues and exercise appropriately the functions allocated to their respective occupational grades.

The first version is inspiring and calculated to achieve enthusiastic cooperation; the second is almost soporific in its effect. It cannot be sufficiently emphasized that the motto for communication, whether written or spoken, should be 'clarity and brevity'.

What kinds of result may be expected from a satisfactory system of communication? Recent studies emphasize the very great practical value of such a system from the point of view of the self-interest of the firm alone, apart from its obvious human desirability. In a lecture in 1965,[1] Dr A. Roberts of Manchester University said, 'effective management demands effective communication as a stern necessity'. He cited several examples of the practical advantages of good systems, for instance:

> An investigation into certain works, some of which had good and some poor systems of communication, showed that those with good systems had fewer disputes, lower labour turnover, and lower absenteeism than those with bad systems.

The point need not be laboured that a large organization needs to have a coherent and carefully thought-out system of communication, to which the same importance is attached as to any of the productive processes. The present inquiry not only deals with the civilized refinements of modern management; it deals with the worker's understanding of technological change.

What has been said so far indicates that this inquiry starts from the following general standpoint: communication is a central activity of industrial leadership which is responsible for stimulating a creative response to the precise imparting of information.

Note: To assist readers it should be noted that for the purposes of this research I have used the designation 'executive' when referring to specific senior staff employed at the Group headquarters. The title 'manager' refers to those in charge of mill operations and sometimes to their immediate subordinates. When the term 'management' is used in a general setting it includes both executives and managers.

[1] At Grimsby College for Further Education, Spring 1965.

2

Background to the study

The Wearwell Group is undoubtedly one of Europe's leading textile manufacturers; references to it in the financial columns of the national press are normally enthusiastic and complimentary.

The headquarters of the Group and almost all the manufacturing units are situated outside urban areas – which means that there are stronger family links and greater social contact between personnel than are found in companies in the larger industrial towns. But these intimate links have been somewhat weakened in recent years as a result of the expansionist policy the firm has followed since 1960. A consideration of the immediate prewar and postwar history of the firm will indicate the nature of its problems.

In the late 1930s the company decided to enter a relatively new field of manufacture. This proved to be a key to prosperity in the immediate postwar years, for the company was able to maintain full production and employment while the rest of the textile industry suffered recession. From 1946 until 1960, the size of the firm remained fairly constant. In 1960, however, when the firm was employing 2,000 people in five separate production units engaged in weaving and yarn preparation, a policy of expansion was initiated. Two firms were then taken over. In 1964 another mill was bought and reopened, and between July of that year and January 1965 eight further firms were taken over. This policy is being continued to the present day.

By the end of 1965, about 10,000 people were employed in

twenty-nine mills all over the textile areas of Great Britain. The size of the units taken over has varied considerably: numbers employed ranged from 200 to 2,000.

The changes that have just been described involved more than the mere expansion of the size of the Group. Among the firms taken over, for instance, were firms of cloth-finishers, yarn-processors, and knitters. The Group has also entered the dyeing trade. Thus diversification of activity has accompanied expansion in size. Weaving, formerly regarded as the dominant activity of the Group, has declined in status as a result of this diversification, particularly through the expansion of yarn-processing.

The somewhat casual nature of the central services provided by the company, at least as regards the personnel management function, was already causing concern to top management by the early 1960s, and by the time the research project was started this anxiety had begun to express itself more frequently and at different levels throughout the Group of companies. The lack of central control and responsibility is seen, for example, in the varying systems of labour recruitment at the mills. At one of the largest mills (referred to as Mill G in the detailed study described in Chapter 4), all job applicants were interviewed by the personnel officer after they had completed an application form. At another mill (Mill F in Chapter 4), the candidates for a job were interviewed by the mill manager. In the first case, an attempt was made to organize the recruitment procedures which were, to some extent, identifiable. In the other case, however, the manager usually took it upon himself personally to see the man 'in the round'. Indeed, if the man seemed suitable for the job, the manager would even drive close to his house to see what type of building it was and whether it looked well kept!

Organizational expansion has had little spectacular influence on the day-to-day working lives of the operatives. Its more obvious effects have been felt to a greater degree by the directors and upper echelons of management. Some of the directors of the old nucleus have had to step down, which they have done graciously; some have had their horizons narrowed by the addition to the organization of abler men; and some have had their positions greatly enhanced. Only a very few operatives have had to change their place of work.

For some managers (both from within the original Group and in firms taken over) the takeovers have simply meant accepting the change from being business competitors in rival firms to being business colleagues working for the same Group.

Some firms taken over have been more radically affected by Group policies, entailing in some cases changes in the trading pattern and even in the higher organizational structure. The yarn-processing firms have, in fact, retained a very high degree of autonomy.

The Group has always, especially in the postwar years, followed a progressive policy regarding the installation of new machinery. Not only has the machinery available been regularly obtained for the mills (and rapid changes have taken place recently in textile machinery), but much has been adapted to fit the very exacting standards of the Group. Moreover, the wide variety of activities carried on at the mills has meant a corresponding diversification of machinery. It is thus clear that technological change, as well as rapid organizational change, must be seen as part of the background to the present inquiry.

The organization chart (p. 16) shows the overall structure of the Group.

The *Main Board* (or Holding Company Board) of the Group is representative of owners of important businesses taken over as well as of the original Wearwell family. It controls the finances of the Group, covering: (a) capital expenditure and working capital and their apportionment to the subsidiaries of the Group; (b) the raising of new capital; (c) distribution of profits. The board determines the policy of the Group in the spheres of personnel relations and public relations so that there is a common approach on the part of each subsidiary. It is also responsible for determining the overall marketing policy of the

WEARWELL CO. LTD
ORGANIZATION CHART
(as at December 1965)

MAIN BOARD *(Holding Company)*

Chairman
Deputy Chairman
Managing Director
Deputy Managing Director
Commercial Director
Financial Director
Director of Overseas Investments
ALTERNATE DIRECTORS
(2 members)
SECRETARY

GROUP SERVICES BOARD

Directors of:
Marketing (Yarns)
Personnel
Marketing
Yarn Supplies & Service
Public Relations, Promotion & Advertising
Project Development
Administration
Quality Control
Management Accounting

GROUP EXECUTIVE BOARD
(10 members)

DIVISION:	EXPORTS	WARP KNITTED	CIRCULAR KNITTED	YARN PROCESSING	FILAMENT WOVEN	WORSTED	COTTON
COMPANY:	A	B	C	D	E	F	G

ENGINEERING

GROUP SERVICES BOARD

Functions:
Advisory
Consultancy service to:
Main Board
Divisional Managing Directors
Specialist Depts
Mill Managers

WEAVING & GREY SALES
Companies H & I
MERCHANTING
Companies J, K, L, M, N, O & P
SURGICAL DRESSINGS
Company Q
DYEING, FINISHING & PRINTING
Companies R, S & T

MAIN BOARD

Functions:
Capital expenditure
Working capital
Raising new capital
Distribution of profits
Overall marketing policy
Public relations
Personnel
Development

GROUP EXECUTIVE BOARD

Functions:
Long- & short-term planning of divisional policy
Coordination of divisions & processes
Day-to-day running of divisions

Group and the long-term planning of the Group's project development.

The *Group Services Board* was set up to assist the Main Board to carry out some of its functions. It includes directors in the fields of marketing, public relations, and management accounting. This board is purely advisory, offering an internal consultancy service to divisional managing directors as well as to the Main Board of directors. The service is either given on request or offered personally by the board members to any of the divisional managing directors, mill managers, or specialists working in the same field as themselves.

The specialists in the mills and divisions look to the Group Services Board for information of a technical character, for advice, and possibly for promotion. On the other hand, they take their daily working instructions from the head of their particular division or company, as the case may be. Regular reports of the work of the specialist directors are given by the Group managing director at the meetings of the Group Executive Board, whose members are expected to pass on the information to their management.

The *Group Executive Board* consists of the heads of the divisions shown on the chart. The deputy managing director of the Group is also on this board, as the managing director of one of the divisions, thus providing a link between this and the Main Board. The chief subsidiary companies – B to G on the organization chart – filament-weaving, yarn-processing, warp-knitted fabrics, circular-knitted fabrics, worsted, and cotton, are completely autonomous, each controlling its own manufacture and sales. Exports (Company A) and the engineering division are equally autonomous. Within the filament-weaving division there are companies – H to T on the organization chart – concerned with dyeing, merchanting, and printing, which fall into a different category: they provide a service and are called upon by other divisions in the Group. On this subject, the managing director of the Group said at a staff conference in March 1965: 'We expect these companies to work very closely with the manufacturing and converting units in achieving greater efficiency.'

An illustration of the work of the three boards in relation to each other may be seen in the case of project development. The director of this service (who is on the Group Services Board) maintains a running survey of new manufacturing trends and new weaving techniques to produce cloth more cheaply. With his colleagues on the Group Services Board he is expected to provide a full economic appraisal of the development of the particular project that will be put to the Main Board for approval. At various times in the preparation of a project, the director of project development has direct liaison with all managing directors of subsidiary companies and, through them, with the industrial research and development sections in each company. Once a project is in production it ceases to be the responsibility of the director of project development and becomes the task of the managing director of the company concerned.

The establishment of the Group Services Board is an example of the sort of measure that a rapidly expanding Group of companies has to take to ensure efficient servicing. It involves the setting-up of a new level of authority and creates new relationships between senior executives. Such complexities inevitably produce problems which affect authority and responsibility, and it is these, particularly as they concern the personnel function, with which this study is concerned.

3

Initial inquiries and report

The Wearwell Group first became interested in using researchers to help to solve its management–employee problems in 1964 after the assistant managing director heard a lecture given by a senior member of the academic staff of the University of Manchester. A series of discussions ensued between the university and the Group and the result was the institution of the present research.

In its early stages the research project encountered several difficulties. There was much confusion about the nature and aims of the research, as Appendix B indicates. Many members of the management team who assisted the researchers were either vague about or entirely ignorant of research methods, and this sometimes damaged cooperation. Moreover, the researchers themselves, though extremely industrious, energetic, and scholarly, were inexperienced, and progress towards drawing conclusions from the vast body of information gathered was slow. Consequently, the Group and the university felt that the appointment of a Senior Research Fellow to supervise the project would overcome many of the difficulties, and I joined the research team nine months after the work had begun.

It seemed to me, at once, that the research lacked a central purpose and that, furthermore, communication between the university and the Group was inadequate in view of the magnitude of the task.

On the second of these difficulties, I was informed by the researchers that they were often unable to obtain information in the Group because a junior executive, whose task it was to link up with the team, had delayed taking action, or had blocked the avenues for consultation with senior executives. The lines of communication between the mill managers and the team were also blurred. The following is an example of the kind of complaint I heard from my colleagues.

They were supposed to be kept informed of any developments in the Group that might affect the research, and yet they had learnt from a casual conversation with a member of the Wearwell staff that a senior executive had set up an important functional committee and was visiting plants to discuss its purpose. The team also expressed doubts about the role of the university authorities in the project. They found it difficult to assess the nature of the relationship between some members of the university staff and the company. My first task was clearly to clarify the roles of all who were directly involved in the research, and to strengthen lines of Wearwell/university communication.[1]

My initial step was to visit as many units within the Group as possible. The purpose of these visits was threefold: I wanted to introduce myself to the senior executives and to explain my function to them; to invite comment on the questions of communication and organizational change; and, unobtrusively, to examine the impact made by the researchers on the Group.[2]

After this series of twenty interviews I prepared a report, and this formed the subject of many long discussions I had with the researchers – individually and collectively – and with the university authorities. Some of the comments in the report caused me to hesitate about making them available to management. However, I decided to make no modifications because to do so might have had the effect of making the reasons for subsequent action seem less urgent. A. T. M. Wilson (1955) has

[1] The importance of the responsibility that the research worker carries is described in a statement published by the British Institute of Management. It is reproduced as Appendix A.

[2] My investigations on the last count had disappointing results, as Appendix B shows. This appendix charts in a brief form my impressions of the reactions of the executives whom I interviewed.

stated the practical side of this problem: 'It seems almost impossible for a social scientist to avoid some degree of responsibility for his activities and for their social consequences.'

Ultimately, the report, with minor additions, was accepted as the basis for the future conduct of the research, and for that reason it is given below in full.

REPORT ON WEARWELL & CO. LTD/ UNIVERSITY OF MANCHESTER PROJECT

The interviews produced information on a variety of matters relating to management development, the authority of the specialist unit, recruitment procedures, and communication in its many, varied forms.

The twenty interviews and discussions were entirely with the more senior management, and were not, therefore, intended to provide a complete statement of the communication systems in the Group of companies – clearly, that would be possible only after a whole series of carefully structured interviews with staff at all levels. An important start to this task has, of course, already been made by the research workers engaged on the project during the past nine months.

AREAS OF DISCUSSION

(a) *The rapid growth of the Group*

Management have no apparent regrets about the aggressive expansionist policy adopted; on the contrary, they seem satisfied with it; but the general impression I formed was that they are concerned that someone should give thought and care to the overall structure of and communication systems in the organization. Several executives feel that communication between the different levels of staff and workers is 'good'. But these executives were not able, in the interviews, to specify why this should be so, except to quote the Wearwell tradition of 'good relations'. Some of them said they were impressed by the way the takeovers were achieved without too many heads rolling – unlike the practice in other parts of the trade and in other industries. 'The takeovers were done by gentlemen,' said one 'taken-over' executive. The majority of the executives were most specific in recognizing the need for a chance to reassess the direction and purpose of the Group. In short, communication between the senior executives and management and between management and workers has been adequate for the operational tasks but it could (and is now beginning to) suffer if proper care is not taken to maintain it as the Group continues to grow.

(b) *Loyalty*

There seems to be considerable loyalty, on the part of management, to the unit or operation with which the individual executive is concerned.

In the opinion of several members of management there is similar loyalty by the employees to the units. To assess whether this loyalty, on the part of both management and works employees, extended to the Group was more difficult. It would seem that no outstanding personality has emerged at top level in the Group to stimulate the sort of loyalty that occurred in the development of other successful firms, such as Plessey and Marks & Spencer.

(c) *The management job*

Surprise was often expressed when I pointed out that the management task would change quite considerably in the next fifteen years, demanding new skills and insights. The changes that most of the executives anticipated were modest and, just occasionally, naïve.

The reasons for the growth of specialist departments in large firms within the last twenty years and more recently in Wearwell were just not understood. Although the top management conference held in March 1965 spelt out the purpose and function of such specialist work and explained the setting-up of a team of Group services, it seems that those who attended the conference did not pass on the information to their staffs, nor have the directors, who comprise this team, been successful in clearly establishing their role in the eyes of the mill managers.

The idea of an extension of management and supervisory training was welcomed by those interviewed. Unfortunately, the enthusiasm was not backed up by any clear understanding of the need to link training with an individual's personal development.

PROPOSALS

(A) To attempt to identify the process of communication as a wholly organizational thing. In other words, to assess the mill manager's attitudes along with those of his subordinate managers and to follow this by a deepening of the research among the employees to discover the effects of top organizational behaviour on communication, effort, and labour relations. Comparisons in organizational behaviour (between the different units) will also be made.

(B) To assess the best means and mechanism for strengthening Group communication, and to establish systems involving actual programmes of personnel and management development in conjunction with the Group Personnel Department.

METHOD

To evolve virtually a new method of inquiry. To get a proper understanding of the organizational behaviour it will be necessary to limit the inquiry to a small number of units. The following will form the basis of the method:

(i) A questionnaire will be given to the managers in two mills, based on the material already obtained in those particular plants as well as in other units. This will be an attempt to check the managers' methods of presenting information.

23

(ii) Shortly afterwards, a research worker will become attached to the manager concerned for a period of *not less than one month*. The replies to the questionnaire will be discussed with the executive not at any one session but over a period of days, say half an hour each morning.

(iii) Research workers will put to supervisors and a sample of operatives a series of questions to be answered daily by the questionnaire method.[1]

I made inquiries outside the Group of companies to ascertain what research of a similar nature was being carried on elsewhere in the textile industry or in other industries. I saw a senior official of the Ministry of Labour at the London headquarters of the Industrial Relations Department. He was helpful within the limits of his experience and after some investigation he informed me that there was no other project to which he or his colleagues in other departments could refer me. He did suggest, however, that I speak to the regional officer of the Ministry in the north-west, and this I did. Again, no related research projects could be traced.

I also made contact with organizations such as the Tavistock Institute of Human Relations, and ascertained, as far as possible, that no research study of a similar character to that taking place in the Wearwell Group was at that time in operation. One other member of the research team made similar inquiries through libraries, university sources, trade associations, and the Shirley Institute, with the same result.

I should say that the answer to my inquiries at the Ministry of Labour was disappointing because I had asked for material past and present, and it appeared that there were no records even of well-known published research on changing situations, like the Tom Burns studies in Scotland referred to earlier.

---

[1] An additional paragraph proposed certain lines of communication between the management in the Group and the university authorities.

4

First study in Mills F and G

It was agreed that the research initiated by the original team before I was appointed to it should be deepened and verified by an examination of attitudes and the communication process in two selected mills. The two mills eventually chosen, which will be called Mills F and G, satisfied a number of criteria agreed upon by the research team and myself.

The quality of communication is often related to (i) the number of people employed in the unit concerned, and to various other considerations which my colleagues and I took into account. They are: (ii) the length of time a mill has been associated with a Group; (iii) the type of process; (iv) the distance of a mill from Group headquarters.

There were insufficient resources available to the project for each of these factors to be considered separately and so it was agreed to select two mills in which factors (i) and (ii) were variable and factors (iii) and (iv) were constant. Thus since Mill F was a small unit and Mill G a large one, since Mill F had come into the Group as the result of the takeover of its parent company only twelve months previously whereas Mill G was one of the Group's original mills, and since the two mills operated a similar production process and were almost equi-distant from Group headquarters, they were selected as the subjects of the proposed intensive study.

During the initial inquiries, described in the previous chapter, among a large number of units within the Group, I gained a very strong impression that the newer members of the Wearwell Group were less satisfied than the older ones with their relations

c

with headquarters and the amount of information they received. It will be remembered that I conducted some twenty interviews among senior management all over the country and that these formed the basis of the report on the state of communications in the Group that I presented to the Wearwell management and to the university. The general tenor of the comments made to me indicated a qualified satisfaction with the Group's expansionist policy and some slight anxiety about the future of communications as a result of this policy.

Most of the unease was on the part of newly taken-over management. For instance, the manager of a mill in Derbyshire, which had been part of the Group for only nine months, said: 'Being taken over was less painful than we had anticipated, but I still feel an outsider. At times there is so little communication from headquarters that I feel they must have forgotten us.' It was also noted in the initial report that there appeared to be considerable loyalty to the individual unit as opposed to the Group. This is, of course, perfectly natural, but thorough and consistent communication on the part of headquarters could transform unit loyalty into dual loyalty, and this would surely be one of its aims.

Furthermore, many of the taken-over companies were small, previously family concerns, where communication had been on a personal and highly informal basis. This tradition appeared to be carrying on in some cases (cf. the manager mentioned in Chapter 2 who visited the street where his job applicants lived in order to assess their living conditions); and while the personal approach is to be commended where it is appropriate, this is hardly the case in a large modern business. These companies were not used to communicating with a parent company and seemed not to have grasped the additional responsibility. Indeed, the parent company itself was at fault in not establishing Group communication procedures in the new firms at the outset.

Thus it was felt that the study of Mills F and G, apart from producing a picture of the communication process in each mill, might reveal differences between these processes which would indicate the factors that had caused such differences to arise. Was it the size of the unit, or the length of its association with the Group, and so on?

Mill F dates back to 1911 when it housed approximately 500 non-automatic weaving looms and had, in addition, accommodation for pre-weaving processes such as warp-sizing and drawing-in, and for cloth inspection, cloth storage, and offices. Around 1927, the building was extended so that it could accommodate 1,200 looms and larger service departments. Apart from the provision of a canteen, no other alterations were made to the building until a new weaving unit was started, early in 1965.

The original product in 1911 was fancy cotton cloth principally for the cotton trade. In the early 1930s 'artificial silk' was introduced, and fiom then on the changeover to viscose yarns was quite rapid so that by the outbreak of war in 1939, when operations were halted by the government and the building was used for storage, production was divided between viscose and secondary acetate fibres. The factory was handed back to the owners in 1946 and production recommenced with the two fibres produced in 1939 until a new man-made yarn became fashionable and manufacture of fabrics from it began to take a share of the overall production. During the last ten years, production has centred on this and the acetate yarns, still supplying cloth mainly for dress, lingerie, and linings outlets.

The original owners were Messrs Walter Smart, who were taken over by Bodley Bros in 1919. The Bodley Bros group of companies continued to expand and to merge until their big merger with the Wearwell Group in 1964. Mill F is now one of the units in Wearwell's filament-weaving division.

The mill is located between two towns in a predominantly cotton-spinning area, being at this time the only weaving unit in the district. This has meant that operatives have normally had to receive weaving training from the company at the commencement of their employment and, because of the decline of the textile industry and general labour conditions, the recruitment of labour has been a main preoccupation of Mill F's management.

At the time of the research, Mill F paid wages that were among the highest in the textile industry and were certainly the highest in the area. This improvement in wages was accompanied by a parallel improvement in conditions and amenities. There were 220 operatives and fifteen staff and supervisors at the mill. In 1965, at a time of large-scale re-equipment of the factory, there was a changeover from day-work to a three-shift system (6 – 2 – 10) spread over five days, which was accepted with very few complaints by the 150 or so employees required to work it.

During the month of the study in Mill F part of the plant was undergoing considerable technological change. Two hundred old looms were to be withdrawn from production and the labour thus released was to be redeployed.

Mill G is one of thirteen weaving units in the Wearwell Group and is situated a few miles to the north of a fairly large Yorkshire town. The building was erected eighty years ago by a company which went out of business in the 1930s. The mill has been a member of the Wearwell Group for twenty years. During the war years the factory was used as a munitions works and the Group took it over in 1946. The type of cloth now produced there is from man-made fibre, and is supplied for lingerie, linings, parachutes, umbrellas, overalls, and industrial outlets. The cloth leaves the factory in the grey state to be finished to customer requirements elsewhere.

The labour force is drawn mainly from two nearby towns and consisted at the time of the research of 200 females and 340 males, plus twenty-four supervisors. Many of the men in the most highly skilled jobs have been working at the mill since the Group took it over – that is, since their demobilization. All employees have enjoyed full-time working (except for a three-day period during the textile depression of 1951) since the mill became part of the Wearwell Group. A three-shift system is worked giving, with Saturday mornings, a $125\frac{1}{2}$-hour week. All employees are members of the appropriate trade unions.

The most senior executive in each of the two mills is the mill manager. Their job descriptions vary very little and, after allowing for operational and structural differences because of the numbers of personnel employed, they have the following common responsibilities:

(a) To ensure that all fabric and goods delivered from the mill meet with the Group quality standard. This includes a target to be aimed at of merchantable production.

(b) To ensure that all departmental supervisors have targets to aim for in budget standards in respect of labour and material costs, and to see that they are met effectively.

(c) To establish and maintain an adequate and well-trained labour force.

(d) To liaise with Group engineering control so as to ensure adequate systematic machine, plant, and building maintenance.

(e) To liaise with the Group personnel and work study staff and, where necessary, with their assistance to negotiate working conditions and wage-rates with the operatives' unions.

The manager's financial responsibilities are limited, since most purchases are made through the director of purchasing at Group level.

METHOD OF INVESTIGATION

I had previously visited both the mills under investigation in order to explain my position and to assess management's reception of the research project. Senior personnel were, therefore, already officially aware of the nature and aims of the research when members of the team arrived at the mills. Nevertheless, it was felt to be important that the purposes and method of the current investigation should be explained in full to each person invited to take part. Discussions were held with the two mill managers before the inception of the new study and an explanation was given to each participant. In addition, a meeting was held in the mill manager's office prior to the start of the survey, to which all concerned were invited. The manager stated the purpose of the study, introduced the questionnaires, and asked for questions. It was explained that the research workers wanted to know the amount, the sources, and the nature of the information the participants received, and, in the case of the mill manager, supervisors, and specialists, how much of it was passed on. During the course of the research, many participants sought the advice of the research workers, particularly on the matter of categorizing information received.

It was agreed that since the information we were seeking was of a numerical nature the questionnaire method of inquiry should be used for ease of tabulation, and that a daily questionnaire should be backed up with at least one interview at which participants might be more inclined to make complaints or to give an indication of what type of information they would like to see increased. The questionnaires would ask (i) how many items of information had been received; (ii) whether they were of a technical, personnel, or general nature; (iii) whether, in the case of the mill manager, they were from other mill managers, headquarters, the unions, mill staff, or other sources; in the case of supervisors and specialists, from the mill manager, colleagues, or other sources; in the case of operatives, from workmates, supervisors, the mill manager, the unions, or other sources, or by the notice board, word of mouth, written statement, or other method; and (iv), except in the case of operatives, how much of the information received had been passed on.

The mill manager at each factory was interviewed on the basis of the questionnaire each day and, since there were only fifteen supervisors and specialists at Mill F and twenty-four at Mill G, it was decided to interview and to give questionnaires to all of them. Of the 220 works employees at Mill F and the 540 at Mill G, samples of twenty and fifty, respectively, were selected, taking into account department, sex, length of service, and shift. This gave a sample of about 9 per cent in each case, which it was felt would be as many as the research team could efficiently cover, bearing in mind that they would be talking to each participant each day, and analysing a daily questionnaire from each participant. The inquiry took place on every working day for four weeks.

A week's supply of the daily questionnaires (reproduced in Appendix C) was distributed at a meeting on a Monday morning and collected the following Monday, and each day each participant had a brief conversation with a research worker to resolve any difficulties that might have arisen. After the four-week period was over, all those involved were interviewed to check the questionnaire answers, to assess whether they felt that the month had been typical, and to assure them that the results would be made available to them. The interviews were unstructured but tended to follow the questionnaire, with additional questions to evaluate satisfaction (see Appendix C, pp. 151–2).

METHOD OF ANALYSIS

Daily records of completed questionnaires were kept for each of the three groups of employees, showing the number of items of information received that day by all employees in that group, the content of the item, the source of the item, and, in the case of the first two categories, how many items were passed on. It had been explained to the participants that they would, no doubt, wish to retain some items of information, but that any information, whether of a technical, personnel, or general nature, that they explained to, discussed with, or simply mentioned to subordinates or peers would need to be recorded.

An example of the daily record for a mill manager is shown in *Table 1*.

Table 1 Daily record for mill manager

| | | Type of information | | | Source of information | | | | | Passed |
Date	Total items	Tech.	Pers.	Gen.	Other MM	HQ	TU	Mill staff	Other	on
Dec. 10	11	9	2	–	–	4	1	6	–	5

At the end of the month these daily records were reduced to summary charts for each group of employees, and conclusions were drawn from them. A monthly summary of the daily record sheets for operatives in Mill G is given in *Table 2*.

Tables 3 to *6* show the overall results for the three categories of employee in both mills. Totals were adjusted slightly before percentages were taken, to take account of daily absenteeism.

Table 3 Summary of patterns of information for mill managers

| Mill | Type of information | | | Source of information | | | | | % passed on |
	Tech.	Pers.	Gen.	Other mill managers	HQ	TU	Mill staff	Other[1]	
	%	%	%	%	%	%	%	%	
F	49	20	31	2	33	1	25	39	77
G	49·4	34·5	16·1	2·4	24·2	3·6	40·8	29	72

Table 4 Summary of patterns of information for supervisors and specialists

| Mill | Type of information | | | Source of information | | | % passed on |
	Tech.	Pers.	Gen.	Mill manager	Col- leagues	Other[1]	
	%	%	%	%	%	%	
F	56	31·5	12·5	22·5	46	31·5	52·5
G	57	16·6	26·4	6·4	49·4	44·2	40·8

[1] 'Other' = manufacturers; outside bodies and contractors; newspapers; people seeking employment at the mill; unspecified 'grapevine' sources.

Table 2 Monthly summary of daily records for operatives – Mill G

Date	Fri. Dec. 10	M 13	T 14	W 15	T 16	F 17	S 18	M 20	T 21	W 22	T 23	F 24	W 29	T 30	F 31	Tues. Jan. 4	W 5	T 6	F 7	S 8
No. of items of inf. received (by all operatives)	90	115	107	132	132	101	17	122	127	138	103	58	116	131	52	128	135	145	127	39
Type																				
technical	57	94	75	92	102	72	10	82	88	100	76	42	85	102	32	93	84	100	90	25
personnel	7	6	11	10	11	12	3	13	16	8	10	12	15	11	10	17	17	11	15	4
general	26	15	21	30	19	17	4	27	23	30	17	4	16	18	10	18	34	34	22	10
Method																				
notice board	9	20	2	18	0	4	0	0	19	4	4	2	15	3	4	26	7	8	2	4
word of mouth	51	76	79	84	96	55	15	77	89	92	73	33	79	78	38	79	91	98	83	32
written statement	21	18	26	29	34	41	2	43	19	40	25	22	22	46	9	23	34	36	40	2
other	9	1	0	1	2	1	0	2	0	2	1	1	0	4	1	0	3	3	2	1
Source																				
workmate	50	75	65	68	70	68	6	72	59	76	66	29	69	63	23	73	78	82	71	23
supervisor	33	36	34	38	32	25	10	40	48	49	26	20	39	51	20	41	41	39	40	13
manager	3	1	0	5	10	6	0	1	1	2	2	3	3	6	2	2	5	7	5	1
trade union	3	0	1	2	1	0	0	0	1	1	0	0	0	1	3	0	2	1	1	0
other	1	3	7	19	19	2	1	9	18	10	9	6	5	10	4	12	9	16	10	2

Table 5 Summary of patterns of information for operatives

| Mill | Type of information | | | Source of information | | | | | Method | | | |
	Tech.	Pers.	Gen.	Work-mates	Super-visors	Mill manager	TU	Other[1]	Notice board	Word of mouth	Written	Other
	%	%	%	%	%	%	%	%	%	%	%	%
F	42	52	6	29·6	42	10	1·4	17	11	77	1	11
G	70·3	10·3	19·4	58	30·3	3	·8	7·9	6·2	68·8	24	1

[1] 'Other' = manufacturers; outside bodies and contractors; newspapers; people seeking employment at the mill; unspecified 'grapevine' sources.

Table 6 Summary of types and amount of information received by three groups of employees

| | Managers | | Supervisors & Specialists | | Operatives | |
	F	G	F	G	F	G
Type of information	%	%	%	%	%	%
technical	49	49·4	56	57	42	70·3
personnel	20	34·5	31·5	16·6	52	10·3
general	31	16·1	12·5	26·4	6	19·4
Average no. of items received per person per day	10·3	18·2	4·7	9·1	2·1	2·14

RESULTS

THE INTERVIEWS

The interviewers attempted to supplement the information obtained from the questionnaires.

They asked the mill managers whether they had been unable to answer any questions put to them, or whether they had asked any questions that could not be answered; whether they had learnt any new fact about the firm in the past twenty-four hours; whether they had learnt anything concerning their work before they entered the mill that morning; and what other methods of communication (e.g. meetings, telephone calls, visits) they had had with headquarters in the past twenty-four hours. Supervisors and specialists were interviewed on similar lines but less frequently than the mill managers, and operatives were interviewed formally only once at the end of the month. In addition to verifying what had been said in the questionnaires, the interviewers asked whether operatives received as much information as they would like and whether what they did receive was relevant and helpful.

The interviews revealed rather more discontent than did the daily questionnaires. Both mill managers felt that they should be receiving more information from headquarters and this in spite of the fact that the manager of Mill G had close contact with many personal friends in head office. This manager was also disappointed at the lack of information emanating from shop-floor level.

It appeared that the two mill managers rarely felt inadequate to answer questions put to them, but the manager at Mill F said that he occasionally referred technical questions to headquarters, and the manager at Mill G had, in the past, referred there one or two questions on personnel matters. Both mill managers had attended a works managers' meeting during the month, which had proved a fruitful source of information, and in Mill F a subsequent internal meeting was held to pass on this information. The manager of Mill G did not run such a meeting, saying that it was unnecessary to do so since he preferred to speak individually to his subordinates. The telephone was clearly the main source of contact between the mill managers and headquarters; letters and visits were very infrequent.

The supervisors and specialists expressed a desire for more information about the scale of operations and basic matters such as the number of mills and the relationships of the divisions to each other.

The operatives were vague about the Group, which prevented them from stating clearly what type of information they wanted about it. But they were anxious to be given more background information, and details of policy and practice in an efficient way.

THE QUESTIONNAIRES

The mill managers

There was an obvious relationship between the patterns of information received by the two mill managers:

1. Half of the total information received by both was of a technical nature.
2. Both passed on between 70 and 80 per cent of the information they received.
3. Both had very little contact with either other mill managers or the trade unions.
4. Both had strong sources of information outside the firm (i.e. 'other').

However, there were some notable differences:

1. The manager of Mill G was more concerned with personnel matters than was the manager at Mill F (34·5 per cent against 20 per cent). He explained that this probably reflected his keen interest in human relations as well as personnel administration.
2. The manager of Mill F depended more on headquarters for his information than did the manager of Mill G (33 per cent of his information originated at headquarters as compared with 24·2 per cent of Mill G's information). In this connection, it should be noted that, during the period of the study, substantial technical changes were taking place at Mill F, producing greater need for contact between this unit and the specialists and top management at headquarters.
3. The manager of Mill G had closer links with his own staff than had the manager of Mill F (40·8 per cent against

25 per cent), a factor borne out by Manager G's stated preference for personal explanation.

4. The manager of Mill G received around eight items of information a day more than did the manager of Mill F.

Supervisors and specialists

Again, there were some striking similarities in the types and sources of information received by supervisors and specialists at the two mills:

1. Over 55 per cent of the total information received by both groups was of a technical nature.

2. Both groups depended heavily on work colleagues for their information. This again indicates the casual nature of the presentation of information.

3. There was only a 12 per cent difference in the pass-on rate, which is small enough to be a monthly variation. In both cases around half the information was passed on.

The differences were:

1. The supervisors and specialists in Mill F received more information from their mill manager than did their counterparts in Mill G (22·5 per cent against 6·4 per cent). The operational changes that took place in Mill F during the month may well have accounted for a closer liaison between these levels of staff.

2. The supervisors and specialists in Mill G made up this deficiency from outside ('other') sources.

3. Of the total information received by supervisors and specialists, a greater proportion concerned personnel matters and a smaller proportion concerned general matters in Mill F as compared with Mill G (31·5 per cent against 16·6 per cent and 12·5 per cent against 26·4 per cent).

4. The supervisors and specialists at Mill G received more information generally than did those at Mill F (9·1 items each day against 4·7).

Communication in an expanding organization
Operatives

Of the three groups of employees, the operatives at the two mills showed the greatest variation in their patterns of information. They were, however, alike in three respects:

1. They received very little information at all (2·1 items per day).
2. There was a very great dependence on information by word of mouth (77 per cent and 68·8 per cent).
3. Both groups received very little information from trade unions (1·4 per cent and ·8 per cent) and from the mill manager (10 per cent and 3 per cent).

The differences between the two sets of operatives were more striking:

1. There was a much greater emphasis on technical information in Mill G compared with Mill F (70·3 per cent against 42 per cent).
2. There was a correspondingly greater emphasis on personnel matters in Mill F as compared with Mill G (52 per cent against 10·3 per cent).
3. Operatives in Mill G depended far more on information from workmates than did operatives in Mill F (58 per cent against 29·6 per cent).
4. There was much more written information given at Mill G than at Mill F (24 per cent against 1 per cent).
5. On the other hand, operatives in Mill F received 10 per cent more information from 'other', mainly outside, sources than did operatives in Mill G.

CONCLUSIONS

1. There was considerable dependence on sources of information outside the firm at managerial and supervisory levels. These sources were in the main newspapers, contractors, and manufacturers. Since managers passed on between 70 and 80

per cent of the information they received, and supervisors and specialists up to 50 per cent, it is obvious that much of what was learnt from these sources was for general dissemination. It would, therefore, surely be an improvement if it were received from more reliable, inside, and formal sources.

2. The channels of communication at operative level were highly informal, being largely word of mouth, the most likely method to produce inaccuracies. Since operatives expressed a wish in the interviews for more information, it is obvious that the lack of formal channels was felt. It is interesting to note how high a proportion of the limited information received by operatives was technical in Mill G and personnel in Mill F, despite the fact that Mill F was in the midst of technical change.

3. While the passing on of information by management, supervisors, and specialists required some stimulation, it should be noted that not all information given to these groups had to be passed on. Certain items (for example, those relating to an operational change) needed to remain with management for a period of time (say three months) before it was politic to refer details of them to supervisors and operatives. At the same time, it could be argued that some of the discontent that operatives felt about their lack of information arose from the reluctance of supervisors to pass on appropriate items of information.

4. There was a need at all levels for more information about the Group and its policies.

5. There were few formal links between the managers of the different mills. Operationally, both Managers F and G had contact with two or three other mills either as an extension of their work or to compare aspects of the various processes. Only a little informal contact was maintained between Mill Manager G and other mill managers, usually by telephone, and even less between Manager F and other mill managers. (It appeared from conversations I had with executives during my initial inquiries (referred to in Chapter 3) that where mills were

involved in joint production there was consequentially closer contact between the managers concerned.)

6. There was little contact between the mills and the trade unions. Where there was a question of rates and services, the matter was handled by a personnel officer at headquarters.

In fact, the only firm conclusion that can be drawn from the above data is that communication in the two mills left a good deal of room for improvement both with regard to the amount of information that was circulated and with regard to its dissemination. There were some variations in the patterns of information received in the two mills, some of which can be accounted for by the particular conditions existing at the time of the study (e.g. during the month of the investigation Mill Manager F had more contact with headquarters than he usually had because a large number of old looms in his mill were being withdrawn from production and the employees thus released were being redeployed), and one or two of which defy explanation (e.g. operatives in Mill F received considerably less technical information than did those in Mill G despite all the technical changes taking place in their mill).

The theory that the size of the unit or the length of its association with the Group is relevant to its communications system was not substantiated by the study, for the general picture produced was one of similarity rather than disparity. The fact that Mill Manager G, who had been employed by the Wearwell Group as head of his unit for twenty years, had strong and satisfactory communication links with headquarters does not emerge. Neither does the difference between the individual styles of communication of the two managers: whereas Manager G used face-to-face methods of communication with his supervisors in an orderly way, Manager F concentrated on personal and somewhat unsystematic attention to detail. Thus Mill Manager G explained to each of his supervisors separately what had passed at the works managers' meeting that took place during the month of the investigation, whereas Manager F held a meeting in his factory for that purpose. On the other hand, Manager F did not inform headquarters that such a meeting had been held (see further comment on the difference in attitude between the two managers in Chapter 6).

There can be no doubt that the overall picture of communication in the two mills was one of informality, where information was largely related to the job in hand and not beyond.

Tentative lines of action are suggested by these research results, even at this stage. There should be a concerted attempt to disseminate more information, particularly of a general nature, about the Group and its policies and plans, to all levels of employees. This could be achieved in a number of ways:

1. By means of regular managerial–supervisory meetings, which should be minuted and at which supervisors should be directed which items they should pass on to their subordinates, preferably in written notices to go on notice boards.
2. By the introduction of a factory edition of a company handbook.
3. By means of regular mill managers' meetings held at Group headquarters and having the same communication responsibilities as the mill managerial–supervisory meetings.

These measures should obviate too great a dependence on outside sources of information and should keep operatives, particularly, better informed.

In addition, it is suggested that, whenever management–union meetings take place to deal with specific issues, the proceedings should be minuted and a summary posted on notice boards.

5

Investigation at head office

While the inquiry at Mills F and G was taking place, the second part of the research began at the Wearwell Group's headquarters, which was itself a symbol of the Group's growth, having expanded rapidly on site as more and more space was required for manufacturing and servicing.

METHOD OF INVESTIGATION

Interviews took place weekly for four weeks with fourteen senior executives, based at headquarters, who had varying degrees of contact with the mills. The interviews provided each executive with an opportunity to answer a questionnaire (P2(4), see Appendix D) and to ask questions about the research project. It was not possible to obtain a 100 per cent response owing to the absence abroad of one executive and the illness of another, so the final number of completed questionnaires represents a 91 per cent response. Fifty-one interviews out of a possible fifty-six were completed.

The questionnaire attempted to identify the kind of information the executives received and distributed according to three main headings, which were explained in some detail to the participants. Before filling in the form each executive was asked to give an example of an item of information to illustrate each of the three categories, so criteria for categorizing information were established at the outset.

As in the study at Mills F and G, information was divided into three main types as follows.

Personnel information

Items relating to human relations and conditions of service within the mill, company headquarters, and Group; for example, information on pay, sickness benefits, holiday allocation, and promotion and training facilities.

Technical information

Items relating to the operations on which the individual was employed, or to the operations that he supervised through his subordinates; matters associated with the improvement of the process, and factors causing possible breakdowns; information involving techniques of production and the actual performance of the individual's job.

General information and plans

Coordination of jobs and processes; the whole range of information necessary for forecasting and for short- and long-term planning; items of general interest, for example from other parts of the Group or from industry in general.

The questionnaire and interviews also attempted to identify the recipients of information disseminated by the executives, and the sources of the information the executives received. Remaining questions covered queries that executives might have been asked and could not answer; those that they might have asked and to which they could obtain no answer; items of completely new information that executives might have gathered about the Group, and the source of these; contact with mill managers; and attendance at meetings.

ANALYSIS OF THE QUESTIONNAIRE RESPONSES

Q.1. Types of information distributed

Thirty-eight of the fifty-one replies revealed that, of the total information distributed by the executives concerned, 15 per cent or less related to personnel matters. In twenty-eight cases, personnel information constituted only 5 per cent or less of the total distributed. For only three executives in the four-week period did information on personnel matters constitute more than 30 per cent of the total information they disseminated, and one of these was a personnel specialist.

Technical information was the main type of information distributed. In the thirty-eight replies mentioned, technical information made up 70 per cent or more of the total information distributed (except in two cases where it was 50 per cent).

The amount of general information disseminated was roughly the same as that of personnel information.

Q.2. Types of information received

The proportion of personnel information in the total amount received was even less than that in the total distributed. For only one executive did the information received contain more than 40 per cent of personnel information, and he was a personnel specialist. Forty-three of the replies showed that personnel information constituted 15 per cent or less of the total information received, and twenty-four replies showed no personnel information at all.

In all but four replies, technical information accounted for 75 per cent of information received.

General information was either slightly more or slightly less than personnel.

Q.3. Recipients of information distributed

The information was distributed to recipients in the following average percentages:

Recipient	%
The mills	44
Other departments at headquarters	19
Outside agencies	22
Deputy managing director and board	15

Q.4. Sources of information received

The sources of information received were as follows:

Source	%
The mills	37
Other departments at headquarters	27
Outside agencies	23
Deputy managing director and board	13

Q.5. Inability to answer questions put by others

Nineteen replies revealed that executives had been asked questions by other executives or staff which they were unable to answer. The topics, and the number of questions relating to each, are listed below:

Category	No.	Topic
Group	9	expansion and development policies
Mill	5	individual mill problems
Job	3	working arrangements
Department	2	departmental plans

Seventeen of the nineteen questions were considered important, in the context of the work situation, by the executives to whom they were addressed. After these executives had pursued the matters raised by the questions with other executives and their superiors, it was anticipated that an answer would be arrived at in eight cases; in the remainder, it was 'doubtful' or 'most unlikely' that a satisfactory answer would be obtained. When I expressed surprise at this result, which suggested a threat to the efficiency of the organization, it was pointed out that the situation arose from the very rapid growth of the Group. 'This wouldn't have happened in the past,' said one long-serving executive, 'but somehow now you are frowned upon if you push a particular query too far.' Two men said that they had genuinely tried to get the answer to a query put to

45

them, only to be told to wait until all the changes had been worked out.

Q.6. Inability to obtain answers to own questions

Fourteen forms produced sixteen questions to which the executives themselves were unable to get answers. The sixteen questions related to the following topics:

Category	No.	Topic
Group	10	expansion, management charts, etc.
Job	4	working arrangements
Mill	2	individual mill problems and coordination

All but two of the sixteen questions were considered important. Obviously, the responses to this item should be seen in conjunction with the responses to item 5 above, which showed that executives to some extent blamed the situation on organizational change.

Q.7. Learning about the organization

On twenty-seven occasions the executives said that they had learnt something entirely new about the organization during the period under review. The information was usually acquired from newspaper reports (especially in the case of takeovers), outside clients, and the company grapevine.

The subjects learnt about in this way, and the number of times they were mentioned, included:

Takeovers and policy (4)
Reorganization of part or whole of the company (7)
Financial position (1)
Group attitude (1)

Speculation about the personalities of the top directors and their families caused some interest (the topic was mentioned on six forms).

It is perhaps surprising that the financial position of the

Group was mentioned only once, especially since the interim dividend was announced during the research period.

During the early part of the month, one of the less senior of the fourteen executives reported that he had heard that a Group management conference was to take place. He was at a loss to pinpoint the source of the information because he thought 'most people knew about it'. In the last week of the period under investigation, three more senior executives mentioned that they had been informed the previous week about a proposed management conference. One of the three executives said that this was 'top confidential' and that he would not have mentioned it had it not been that I was engaged in a research capacity. The other two executives said that they had been told about the conference at a luncheon with their chief. The remaining ten executives did not report on this information at all and in the subsequent talks with them it appeared that only two of them knew about the proposed conference. Both said that they had not mentioned it during the month because they had been given the information just before the month of reporting had begun, a perfectly reasonable attitude, given our terms of reference.

Q.8. Methods of communication

Contact between the executives and the mill managers was expressed in terms of the time taken up by three methods of communication:

Method	%
Visits	12
Telephone	56
Letters	32

For the purposes of this calculation executives were instructed to record a *visit* simply as the time it took, four *telephone calls* as one-quarter of a day, and four *letters* as one-quarter of a day.

Q.9. Attendance at meetings

Eleven executives attended an average of three formal meetings each during the period. The nature of these meetings, and their frequency, are shown below:

> Operational meetings
> (relating to a specific problem in a mill) (2)
> General production meetings (7)
> Meetings outside the Group (3)

Executives also attended a few small informal meetings.

The operational meetings usually involved the individual executive representing the Group responsibility, together with the mill manager and his immediate subordinate.

General production meetings were usually gatherings of one senior executive and the managers of the filament-weaving division, or those managers responsible for the installation of a new process or the modification of an old one.

Meetings outside the Group were those involving community activities or they were district or regional meetings of trade or management bodies.

DISCUSSION OF RESULTS

Executives gave and received very little personnel information indeed; they did, however, obtain and pass on a large number of technical data.

A higher degree of contact was maintained with the mills than with any of the other sources or recipients of information. The distribution of 44 per cent of information to the mills (Q.3) and the receipt of 37 per cent of information from the mills (Q.4) do not mean, however, that executives were in touch with all mills to the same extent, but rather that much contact was likely to be made with a few mills. Circumstances may have forced an executive to keep in touch with one particular mill far more than with others, because, for instance, of a loom change. But the differences between the mills in respect of the amount of contact they had with executives at headquarters were quite striking, and our inquiries revealed that mills not in such close touch with these executives resented their lack of communication. Executive E, in an interview (referred to later), said that he had just come from a mill manager new to the Group who had told him: 'Mr —— (a manager of a mill long associated with the Group) has made his second visit to headquarters within a month. What I'd like to know is why he should be there and whether he's a blue-eyed boy.' There may have been, of course, a perfectly valid explanation for any such visit. If the communication system, particularly for the newer firms in the Group, was efficient, each manager would appreciate the Group's intentions regarding his mill and its inter-relationships (if any) with other mills, and regarding himself, and suspicion would not arise to the same extent.

The replies to Q.5 (inability to answer questions) and Q.6 (inability to obtain answers) revealed that between 31 and 37 per cent of executives were uncertain of always being able to get answers to matters that they considered to be important. The executives themselves blamed this state of affairs on organizational change; indeed, there was almost an attitude that lack of communication is endemic in change.

The answers to Q.7 (learning about the organization) showed just how interested executives were in individual personalities within the firm. Six executives showed great interest and some anxiety about the roles to be performed by top executives and their families. When several old family firms were taken over, some of the family directors had to be accommodated. This provided a constant talking-point at all levels, but particularly among the executives at headquarters.

Three striking features should be noted from this analysis of the questionnaire responses.

The first point is the imbalance between the amounts of technical, personnel, and general information both received and distributed by the executives, particularly if we recall the definition of 'technical' that was used, i.e. information dealing with local or isolated problems. Because this is the textile trade it is accepted that there would be almost daily minor changes of a technical nature to meet individual customers' requirements, and these would entail items of technical information. What is most noticeable is the lack of personnel and general information (the latter being concerned with policy matters and long-term planning).

Second, executives obtained a large amount of new and original information dealing with the expansion and development of the Group from outside, mainly from newspapers. In view of the fact that the popular press does not carry a great deal of city and business news it is obviously essential to be reading *The Guardian*, *The Financial Times*, or *The Times*!

Third, the replies to Q.7 showed that the passing of information was not related to levels of authority. The classical concept of management theory, which sees information passing down a chain of command, has to be put alongside the comments made here. That a management conference had been proposed was an important piece of information; in fact, it required particularly careful handling in view of the highly restricted list of executives invited to attend the previous conference (this incident will be described in detail in the final section of this chapter, pp. 63–8). But their responses revealed that these fourteen executives at headquarters – at varying levels but all fairly senior – were informed of the conference at widely differing times, if at all, and with little regard to seniority.

Because the mills were scattered over a wide area, it is only to be expected that letters and telephone calls should account for nearly 90 per cent of the time taken in communication between headquarters and the mills. Yet dependence on these methods places increasing responsibility on the mill manager in a rapidly expanding company to get across to senior executives and specialists at headquarters the grass-roots problems of their work. Without the benefit of full discussion, letters and telephone calls certainly create a sense of urgency but not the feeling of a working environment. They could lead to decisions being taken at headquarters without full understanding of shop-floor practice or the particular circumstances of each case, a state of affairs that was bemoaned by Mill Managers F and G in the follow-up described in Chapter 6.

An average of three meetings in a month does not seem very high for a firm undergoing such extensive organizational change.

Perhaps no further comment is necessary, but, in private conversation, executives made it plain to me that they had scant regard for meetings, which were considered to be an inadequate way of getting decisions made. I am tolerant of this view to some extent because it reflects the uncertainties in the minds of the management personnel about doing things differently from the way in which they were done in the past when, for most of them, operations were on a smaller scale and no such meetings were required. However, the same executives who talked about unnecessary committees were among those who criticized the lack of communication in the Group. They had not been encouraged to think of meetings as a valuable communication technique.

ANALYSIS OF THE INTERVIEWS

The interviews were conducted in a friendly, informal atmosphere, in which the interviewer showed himself willing to give information as well as to receive it, an approach advocated by Cicourel (1964).

Summaries of the main points made by executives at the interviews are given below. The rating refers to the score out of 100 that the particular executive gave to communication in the Group.

Rating score

The executives were invited to give a rating for Group communication, after the following scores had been explained to them:

0–25: Very poor. Complete lack of purpose within the organization. No objectives or targets stated by top management.

25–50: Poor. Morale poor. Little attempt to understand other departments and sectional work.

50–75: Average. The quality of the information varies. Although at times things are good, the variations are upsetting and cause conflict.

75–100: Good. Care is taken by top executives to keep management and staff adequately informed.

100: Excellent. A perfect working environment to aim for rather than achieve. No conflict and adequate consultation throughout.

EXECUTIVE A

Service with the company: more than twenty years.
Responsibilities: Group-wide.

'Communication is fairly good, but there are acute human relations problems arising from the rapid growth of the Group. For example, I used to see the managing director daily to deal with work problems. In recent years this practice has stopped. When I do see him (and during work this is rare) it is for a mere twenty seconds.

I manage to keep in touch with the goings-on in the company by my membership of the local golf club. Only last Saturday, I learnt of the future policy of the company at a dinner party attended by company executives among others. I consider this to be only partly adequate.'

Suggestion

'A monthly news-sheet should be published, dealing with all aspects of company functions. Brief, to the point, such a document would provide the same sort of facilities as the current marketing news-sheet prepared by a member of the company's sales office.'

Rating: 60.

EXECUTIVE B

Service with the company: more than twenty years.
Responsibilities: Group-wide.

'Communication is bad – couldn't be worse. Indeed, it has never been worse. In a long association with the company I am surprised to find that communication at all levels is so vague and uncertain. The top executives just seem unable to deal with the needs and interests of all those people below them. I would like to know who is *really* responsible for training and succession.' (See final section of this chapter, p. 63.)

Suggestions

'(a) A management organization chart for the whole of the filament division.
(b) Top executives should, through training courses, be made to see just how they can affect employee attitudes. They should be encouraged to explain and record decisions, when these are not confidential, to prevent the grapevine taking over what is their job.
(c) Memos should be sent out when executive changes have taken place. I didn't know about two major changes that took place recently. I was eventually told, first by an outsider, then by the grapevine.'

Rating: 35.

EXECUTIVE C

Service with the company: more than twenty years.
Responsibilities: divisional.

'Communication can and must improve. I reported in the questionnaire that during the working week there were questions put to me that I was unable to answer. I consider this to be an indication of the changing circumstances and growth of the company. For instance, new systems and new

53

machinery cause personnel to ask for help and advice to a greater extent than in the past. I am fairly successful at establishing good relations with mill managers, but they do not welcome change and could prove difficult with a more aggressive coordinator.'

Suggestions

'(a) Good communication starts at the top. If the top executives don't understand this point, then the actual messages and instructions they are responsible for will become even more distorted and meaningless lower down.
(b) Strengthen the line of command and encourage all levels to pass on information promptly. At the moment the actual lines of authority are very unclear.'

Rating: 40.

EXECUTIVE D

Service with the company: more than twenty years.
Responsibilities: Group-wide.

'Breakdowns in communication occur because of the size of the new operations. For instance, I discovered when visiting one distant plant about the change of process affecting X town and Y town. I still have not heard officially about this and yet it will pose great problems for me. I feel sorry for Senior Executive Q [newly promoted] because I don't know what he is supposed to be doing nor do any of us.' (See final section of this chapter, p. 63.)

Suggestion

'Greater authority should be given to the line manager to take up his communication task, which is to keep people in touch with what is happening. In this way, cooperation and better attitudes will develop.'

Rating: 55.

EXECUTIVE E

Service with the company: five–ten years.
Responsibilities: divisional.

'Communication has deteriorated during the expansion of the company. I do not have access to information outside the company. I rely entirely on my chief. Nobody seems to take too much notice of what is said and when it is said. I am no longer certain of the duties of several of our senior people.' (See the final section of this chapter, p. 63.)

Suggestion

'Job descriptions would help so that management and staff would get to know their job limits as well as having an idea of other people's responsibilities. In an expanding company, I suggest that a job description is particularly important.'

Rating: 50.

EXECUTIVE F

Service with the company: five–ten years.
Responsibilities: divisional.

'The organization is changing so quickly that it is not always possible to tell who has the responsibility for a particular action. At the same time, it is difficult to get to the top executive. It looks as if he needs someone to help him and ensure that decision-making is prompt and effective.

An example of poor communication and bad personnel administration was the handling of the profit-sharing scheme. This was prepared two years ago, but no formal or informal statement has yet been issued on the matter. Within the past fortnight, two groups of workers in different towns have asked what has happened to the profit-sharing scheme. One union official asked whether it had been introduced elsewhere in the company. They were worried that they had been overlooked by the company.'

Suggestion

'Because of the errors involved in the process of spoken communication, on which so many people fall down, I would advocate that memos should be used more effectively between management and other branches of management, and between management and specialists.'

Rating: 50 – probably less.

EXECUTIVE G

Service with the company: more than twenty years.
Responsibilities: Group-wide.

'I don't think communication is quite so bad in those parts of the business that have been part of the Wearwell Group from the beginning. I do hear from the managers concerned in the newer parts that we have taken over that they don't know what's going on, and it would be a mistake for us older members to think they don't care. They do care – if for no other reason than that their future depends on it.'

Suggestion

'None – it's up to the managing director to decide what to do.'

Rating: 50.

EXECUTIVE H

Service with the company: more than twenty years.
Responsibilities: Group-wide.

'Communication has been discussed so often at meetings that I regard both management and staff at headquarters to be too blasé about it. As a matter of fact, when communications are discussed in my presence, the discussion tends to become frivolous. One of the reasons for poor communication is that many people do not have the experience or the understanding to get in touch with other people to ask for advice and information. Communication will always need improvement because people are naturally curious as to what is going on in their working environment.'

Suggestions

'(a) Improvements in communication can only be brought about by the outside professional consultant or adviser who can observe, record, and report the information process which already exists.

(b) Each executive has a special responsibility to examine what information he needs and then to go to the appropriate person and ask for it. Top management should go outside their immediate office and find out what they need to make their work more effective. Unfortunately, I am seldom asked for my advice so that a lot of the information that I have access to is not properly utilized. Also, in the big firm we are now, you feel there's no point in making a fuss about what you do know. I'm afraid you wait for people to come to you.

(c) If the twelve Wearwell directors were really to cooperate and show their staffs and colleagues that they were keen to do so, morale would improve throughout the whole organization.'

Rating: 50.

EXECUTIVE I

Service with the company: more than twenty years.
Responsibilities: divisional.

'Communication is fairly good as far as I'm concerned. By that I mean that my own contacts with my staff and their contacts with each other are good. Communication within the Group is rather poor. Not enough people know what is happening or likely to happen. There is no clear statement of fringe benefits for executives and no attempt to explain the subtleties of status between the different levels of authority. I would like to know what Executive Q does here.' (See final section of this chapter, p. 63.)

Suggestions

'(a) Formal meetings between the directors and immediately subordinate levels of management should be encouraged. They need not be regular or long-winded.

(b) Coordinate the suggestions that follow from the big management and staff conferences. Staff like to feel that what they have proposed is not forgotten.' (See final section of this chapter for details of such a conference.)

Rating: 50.

EXECUTIVE J

Service with the company: more than twenty years.
Responsibilities: Group-wide.

'The rapid expansion within the organization must cause changes in cooperation, morale, and the way people work together generally. All this means that communication has inevitably been affected.

The different philosophies of the companies taken over must also influence the information flow. Do we know enough about these philosophies and the different ways of doing things in the other companies?

Unfortunately, most of us senior executives simply haven't had the opportunity to examine and assess the total growth of the Group.'

Suggestions

'(a) Research: The fact that the company has arranged to give facilities to a university research team to examine communication suggests that some of the solutions are being sought.

(b) Conferences: A Group conference in which management and staff are brought together for a few days must go some way to helping people to identify each other – to see each other as human beings.

(c) The actual message: More important than the method of communication is the actual message being conveyed. People want to know what is happening within the organization and when *they* may receive training and where *their* future lies, etc.'

Rating: 75.

EXECUTIVE K

Service with the company: more than twenty years.
Responsibilities: Group-wide.

'Good communication is lacking at all levels. I can get information and some answers to problems from sources that I should not have access to. At the same time, my staff often come to me and ask, "Is this correct?" or "Is so and so going to happen?" and I cannot help them. How the other people get their information is beyond me but it causes anxiety to all concerned. We must not ignore the way the grapevine works; everyone has an interest in finding out what is likely to happen to the company and through the company to themselves, and they will do so somehow.'

Suggestions

'(a) Discipline – not in an authoritarian sense – should operate, so that managers and supervisors report back more accurately and effectively to their colleagues and subordinates. "Don't leave it to chance" should be the motto of all senior executives in handling information.

(b) There should be more written rather than spoken information. Since the expansion of Wearwell, there has been a great increase in messages by word of mouth, which means that the instruction or advice is less reliable because it has to filter down or across from a particular sector of the business.

(c) Properly designed management training courses would go some way towards improving the way people cooperate with each other in the mills.'

Rating: 40.

EXECUTIVE L

Service with the company: five–ten years.
Responsibilities: Group-wide.

'Communications could be improved. A recent Group conference revealed the need for more information. Organization and management charts are badly needed.

Employees at all levels ask, "What is going on?" This is particularly true of the junior staff, who are greatly interested in the way the company will move in the future.

The conference held recently has encouraged staff to feel better about the company. To avoid frustration setting in, this needs to be maintained.'

Suggestions

'(a) A news bulletin, simple and effective, would help to make people feel part of the overall organization.
(b) Discussion groups (without executive authority) would stimulate the flow of ideas. Care should be taken to ensure that these were not meetings encouraging moans. They should cut across management ranks. The participants at the meetings should be expected to report back to their staffs.
(c) Although it is making a contribution in certain directions, the Group Services Board[1] is not completely effective. It has no teeth. One difficulty is its tendency, encouraged by top executives, to try not to upset the local managing directors.'

Rating: 50.

[1] The setting-up of this board s referred to in the final section of this chapter.

EXECUTIVE M[1]

Service with the company: more than twenty years.
Responsibilities: divisional.

'Communication has deteriorated with the rapid expansion of the company recently. For instance, the sales offices in London feel less a part of the organization now because of the growth of the manufacturing units.'

Suggestions

'(a) More personal contact. It should be the aim of all management to be more informal with staff.

(b) An effective organization structure would help to clarify roles and responsibilities. I don't mean simply having charts and diagrams about the place.

(c) A strong and comprehensive personnel policy for the filament-weaving division. This could, for instance, assist the youngster who has just joined the firm by providing a training course which would facilitate a proper adjustment to the job. Opportunities must also be provided to develop senior executives properly.'

Rating: 50.

EXECUTIVE N

Service with the company: more than twenty years.
Responsibilities: Group-wide.

'Communication is not good. People think that communication and morale will improve by simply sending a letter or making a telephone call to put something right. There is no conception of teamwork and the improvement of communication by effort and *esprit de corps*. The whole question of

[1] This executive has a liaison function since he deals with inquiries made to the sales offices of the Group in London. Inquiries from customers are mainly dealt with in London but considerable reference is made to Executive M.

team spirit needs driving home at all levels, particularly by the Main Board.

Uncertainty about the individual manager's future between Wearwell's and one of the companies taken over has arisen because of lack of clarity in messages and policy statements affecting the merger.'

Suggestions

'(a) The Group Services Board cannot cope with the increasing needs of the manufacturing units; more staff are needed.

(b) Supervisory and management tasks could be made so much easier if full training facilities were provided and if these were regarded as part of the individual staff member's development.

(c) Teamwork is the important way to develop morale. Newsletters and conferences can only act as poor substitutes.'

Rating: 40.

POINTS ARISING FROM THE INTERVIEWS

It is not intended to make a categorical assertion at this stage, but it would seem that a rating for communication of below 50 is unsatisfactory, and that 75 should be aimed at. Since only one executive gave communication in the firm a rating of 75, it is concluded that the executives interviewed were almost unanimous in feeling that there was substantial room for improvement in the system of communication in the Group. The average rating for the fourteen executives was 49·5.

The effects of this situation as stated or implied in the interviews are worth noting: bewilderment, ignorance, frustration, and insecurity cause a widespread crumbling of morale.

The executives were almost unanimous also in tracing the cause of the inadequate communication to the recent expansion of the firm.

There was emphasis on the damaging effect of having to rely on informal, haphazard, and grapevine sources.

There was a reiteration of the overriding responsibility of top executives to ensure a satisfactory system of communication. The various suggestions deserve attention, in particular the following: news-sheets, strengthened lines of command, training courses, memoranda, organization charts, consultants and researchers, meetings and conferences, training courses, job descriptions, coordination and follow-up, personal contact, more staff, a comprehensive personnel policy.

Some of these points will be expanded later.

'*The Case of the Unknown Management Conference Report*'

A number of executives commented that they did not understand the duties of certain senior executives. In addition to the statements quoted here, which were made in a controlled setting, a large number of these and other executives made similar comments even more forcibly in conversation. At the same time there was a general, rather confused feeling that executives should be appointed to put various organizational ills to rights.

An example of an obvious breakdown of coordination with regard to the creation of new jobs, organizational change, and the personalities involved was vividly provided by what can only be described as 'The Case of the Unknown Management Conference Report'. Nearly a year before this particular part of the investigation took place, the Group ran a management conference which included about fifty of its top executives. It was residential and took place in a seaside town near to the headquarters. The 'Who's Who' revealed representatives of the Main Board: the chairman, deputy chairman, and managing director, as well as the top executives of the individual companies which had been taken over. This was not the first company conference but it was much more selective in its representation than were those held on previous occasions. At the commencement of the conference, the managing director of Wearwell's announced a new allocation of titles and jobs under the heading of 'The Group structure'. He announced that the Main (Holding) Board would determine the policy of the Group in the spheres of marketing, project development, personnel relations, and public relations 'so that there is a common approach throughout by each subsidiary'. The managing director then went on to say that, to enable the board to carry out its functions, a team would be set up to be responsible for Group services, covering the functions mentioned and others related to them. The names of the new directors and their functions were given.

Later in the conference the participants were left in no doubt about the changes and about the people who would be charged with the new duties. Let us take one example, that of the director of personnel and training:[1] the deputy managing director provided, in his lecture, a detailed job description, as follows:

'He [the personnel director] will be responsible to the managing director, and will develop a system of liaison and coordination between the Group Services Board and the divisional boards, aiming at the optimum use of our resources in manpower.

The great problem in British industry today is to provide adequate management, not so much specialists, but general management, and Mr —— will endeavour to fulfil this Group's requirements in years to come.

Not even the most thorough and comprehensive forecasts can ensure that we foresee our managerial requirements exactly, but we can minimize our future difficulties by an enlightened systematic management development programme.

We must ensure that Group opportunities are known and we must review our current approaches to ensure that we have adequate trained coverage for all key positions. We

[1] Referred to in the interviews as Executive Q.

64

must see that, where necessary, potential managers and management supervisory trainees are strategically placed, working in responsible positions with established managers or executives at both Group and divisional levels. Such "training with responsibility", designed to keep the trainees in touch with the realities of management, correctly assessed, will allow these individuals to gain a broad basic understanding of business and management and will improve the value of people as the company's most important asset.

On general matters he will assist in the formulation of revised company policy designed to meet changing requirements, develop and maintain methods of getting this fully understood and accepted throughout the Group, and recommend revisions when policy is not in line with up-to-date thinking. It is important that trust in management and understanding of company objectives and policies should be the aims at all times.

In the evaluation of the current Group position he will assess the present policies of companies in the Group relative to personnel, seek out anomalies, and recommend appropriate action to eliminate them.

With regard to the selection and recruitment of personnel he will evaluate methods of recruitment, determine requirements within the Group, and collaborate with appropriate executives to fulfil these requirements.

The induction of personnel into the Group needs careful study to ensure that the correct approach is made to all categories: school-leavers, apprentices, graduates, personnel from other organizations; and to ensure adherence to the Contracts of Employment Act, 1963.

I have mentioned previously the training of managerial and executive staff. This will also apply to supervisors and operatives and, with regard to the latter, it will fall in line with the Industrial Training Act.

With regard to promotion and succession, I have spoken of this also, but, additionally, Mr —— will encourage further education and will plan courses and seminars at all levels of employment.

Our strength in the past has been very generally associated with an adequate training of operatives and supervisors by the well-known TWI[1] methods, designed and developed to suit our own particular needs; these will be revised to take into account new techniques.

To ensure equitable wages and salary administration, Mr —— will maintain adequate current information on scales in use, evaluate alternative methods of wages payments, and recommend new structures when advisable.

He will arrange to promote training for safety and accident prevention, and the appropriate services for health; liaise with external organizations such as factory inspectors, Ministry of Labour officials, educational organizations, and training establishments; and advise in negotiations with trade unions and employers' associations, but I must stress the word *advise* in this respect. He will not normally enter into negotiations on behalf of any company within the Group.

The subject of fringe benefits looms very large in our eyes today and Mr —— will ascertain variations in fringe benefits now operating in different companies in the Group and will seek to get uniformity in this respect. He will also evaluate new trends, and there are many such trends emerging in business today.

It is our wish that a common policy throughout the Group should exist in relation to conditions of employment, including pensions, fringe benefits, holiday arrangements, etc., and Mr —— will endeavour to apply a common policy. He will assist in special projects such as: re-location of production facilities, cost of labour turnover, suggestion schemes, and attitude surveys.'

Despite the wide-ranging activities included in this job description, nine months to a year later there had been no

[1] Training within Industry.

obvious discoverable attempt to convey knowledge of them to staff or employees in the mills. The research team made a number of inquiries about the conference but it was only as a result of a private conversation in a bar with an executive that I discovered that a report of it had been issued. I asked the man whether I could see it. He agreed, on condition that I mentioned to nobody his name, since he had 'borrowed' a copy; as far as he knew, 'the circulation was confined to those attending'. Attempts to check this confirmed that it was extremely difficult to discover exactly to whom the report *had* been distributed. A balance of the evidence from all the comments of executives and staff suggests that it had a fairly restricted distribution. But more important than the inadequate distribution of the conference report was the apparent inability of those on the Main Board, and those who were affected by the decisions it contained, to communicate what had happened to the thousands of employees who were not at the conference.

Hence, the comments made by executives in this head-office inquiry show that fairly senior decision-makers in Wearwell's were not clear about the role and responsibility of an executive nine months to a year after a Group-wide conference had taken place giving details of both.

The particular executive whose job is described above told me that he was finding it difficult to establish himself and his job, a reflection of the failure of Main Board members to establish proper contact with their subordinates. It is conceivable, in view of the importance of the mill managers in circulating Group information, that had they had a precise discussion on the changes to be made shortly after the conference had taken place, the subsequent misunderstandings could have been avoided.

One final word on the missing conference report. Since the research team had not been informed about it (and it should be noted that my assistants were actually on the spot when the conference took place, before I arrived) there was great enthusiasm when I finally produced my copy of the proceedings.

The other members of the research team then tried to obtain copies through various channels within the organization, but without success. Furthermore, a senior member of the university staff, who was a consultant to the Group as well as an adviser to the research team, was unaware of the report's existence.

6

Follow-up in Mills F and G

It was decided that the responses given during the inquiry in Mills F and G should be checked two months later to assess any alteration in attitudes and to gauge the reaction of the original participants to a summary of the collective views expressed (see Appendix E for summary statements and questionnaires).

It was noted in Chapter 4 that Mill Manager G received virtually twice as much information as Manager F. This difference was reflected in the amount of information circulating at supervisory level in the two mills, for the daily amount of information received at this level was considerably higher in Mill G than in Mill F. It was hoped that the follow-up would discover whether there was a tendency in organizational behaviour towards either inhibiting or easing the flow of information.

METHOD

I approached the mill managers personally, explaining that it was not intended to have a further detailed study lasting a month (in case they were daunted at the thought of another lengthy project so soon) and that I had only two requirements: first, to be able to make available to the original participants copies of the summary of the findings of the earlier study; and, second, to be allowed to invite them to comment on the material. I would personally explain the exercise to the employees.

The mill managers approved my plans and agreed on times for me to cover the various shifts.

The participants were seen in small groups of twos and threes, when they read the summary statement and made comments by means of a questionnaire. I again impressed upon them that this was a personal exercise between myself (representing the university) and them. They should feel free to withdraw from the exercise at that time if they had any doubt about the integrity of the work involved. Possibly because I took pains to clarify this to the employees and to stimulate comment and criticism, agreement to cooperate was unanimous. Comments on leaving the meetings ranged from 'Glad to help you, Mr Moonshine' to 'If we do this then, will we not see you again?'

The summary of the findings of the research on communication among operatives (Appendix E, p. 156) was given to all participants. The statement on supervisors (p. 155) was given only to the supervisors, specialists, and mill managers. Questionnaire P3 (see pp. 156–7) was given to operatives, and Questionnaire P3(1) (see pp. 158–9) to supervisors and specialists. The managers were not given a questionnaire but were invited to make comments in an interview, if they chose to.

To ensure that all the participants were clear about the intentions of this stage of the project, I covered every shift and discussed the study with those involved in it in the manner described earlier. Workers on the night-shift were seen between 10 p.m., when the shift started, and midnight.

MILL F

SUPERVISORS AND SPECIALISTS (15)

Q.1. Categories of information

(a) Does the range of information received by supervisors in your mill and described in the statement you have just read

	%
surprise you?	7
confirm your previous views?	86
have no interest for you?	7

(b) Do you consider the relative percentage of each category of information satisfactory or not? Give reasons.

	%
Yes	50
No	23
Doubtful	7
Did not reply	20

(c) Have you any comments to make on the amount of information received by supervisors at the other mill in the research project?

Fifteen per cent made some comment. The supervisors, in most cases, offered a quantitative assessment, since only three had any practical knowledge of the other mill.

The most persistent statement was that supervisors at all mills should receive the same information and that it should come from the Group or top executives.

Q.2. Sources of information

(a) Does the breakdown of the sources of information in your mill

	%
surprise you?	21·5
confirm your previous views?	71·5
have no interest for you?	7

(b) Have you any comments to make on the sources of information available to the supervisors in your mill?

Sixty per cent replied to this question and the answers were divided fairly equally into three categories:

(i) The information we get within the mill is all right but contact from the Group is poor and unclear.

(ii) A smoother process for telling people what is happening is needed at all levels.

(iii) More formality is needed.

Q.3. Information retained

Does the amount of information retained by supervisors in your mill

	%
surprise you?	7
confirm your previous views?	86
have no interest for you?	7

Q.4. More information required

(a) The need for more information was expressed by supervisors in your mill. Does this

	%
surprise you?	21·5
confirm your previous views?	71·5
have no interest for you?	7

(b) State the type of information, if any, of which you feel you get too much.

None   75%

The remainder answered that they received too many pieces of gossip, 'tell-tales', etc.

(c) State the type of information, if any, of which you feel you do not get enough.

See additional comments below.

Q.5. Replies from operatives

(a) Do the replies of the employees in your mill

	%
surprise you?	17
confirm your previous views?	70
have no interest for you?	13

(b) Have you any comments to make on their replies?

See additional comments below.

Additional comments

Questions 4(c) and 5(b) were open-ended and provided some interesting detailed replies.

Q.4(c): State the type of information, if any, of which you feel you do not get enough.

Summary of replies:

	%
Technical	45·7
Wearwell (and Group activities)	36·3
Future planning	18

More specifically:

'What's happening at the top?'

'Information from outside sources, i.e. after-sales information, new plant and equipment. Management does not give a straight answer and quite often the ball is thrown back at me.'

'An official list of HQ departments with names of people to contact would be helpful.'

'Information to follow up any changes, etc. concerning the job that may have occurred since leaving work until return next day.'

'The important thing is not how much we get but *when* we get it.'

Q.5(b): Have you any comments to make on their [the operatives'] replies?

Summary of replies:

A more scattered range of comments was recorded, with the following occurring most frequently:

	%
Reasonable	25
The criticism is due to discontent	20
Those who are critical don't stay too long in Wearwell's	20

More specifically:

'The method of transmitting information by word of mouth is outdated. We don't get to know why something is happening – we just get to know when.'

'Not able to – I could tell plenty.'

'I try to inform all my employees.'

'Nobody would think of asking me about company plans and the future policy of Wearwell.'

'Although two items per day seems reasonable I would have thought that the other mill's figure would have been greater than our mill's because of the introduction of new working conditions.'

'Ninety per cent of the information I get has no bearing on what I'm doing.'

OPERATIVES (20)

Q.1. Categories of information

(a) Does the amount of information received by your fellow-operatives in your mill, and described in the statement you have just read

	%
surprise you?	18
confirm your previous views?	82
have no interest for you?	0

(b) Do you consider the amount of information in each category satisfactory or not? Give reasons.

	%
Yes	60
No	40

(c) Have you any comments to make on the amount of information received by employees at the other mill in the research project?

Of the replies given, which could only be a quantitative comparison by operatives, the following occurred most frequently:

	%
The other mill seems better informed	25
All mills need more technical information	15
I wish I knew something about the other mill	20

See additional comments, p. 76.

Q.2. Sources of information

(a) Seventy-seven per cent of the information received is by word of mouth from supervisors and your other workmates. Does this figure

	%
surprise you?	0
confirm your previous views?	90
have no interest for you?	10

(b) Have you any comments to make on how other sources of information might be used to help you in your work?

Ninety per cent offered suggestions, including the following:

	%
Regular meetings (formal, 'with a purpose')	50
Bulletins (works newspapers)	30
Better supervision	10

See additional comments, p. 77.

75

Q.3. More information required

(a) The need for more information was expressed by employees in your mill. Does this

	%
surprise you?	
confirm your previous view?	100
have no interest for you?	

(b) State the type of information, if any, of which you feel you get too much.

	%
None	63·7
Informal or grapevine	36·3

(c) State the type of information, if any, of which you feel you do not get enough.

	%
Technical	50
Wearwell	40
Financial	10

See additional comments below.

Additional comments

Q.1: Amount and categories of information, and comments about other mill.

'This information business has been a bit of a laugh. During the research worker's visits we received lots and lots of news. Since his departure – not a word.'

'More technical information could be passed on to the worker in writing, e.g. booklets and pamphlets which machine manufacturers publish about new methods. If the books are in short supply, why not a summary of the instructions?'

'We never know whether the information we get is fact or not – it's too casual.'

'To be quite honest, I had not even heard that the other mill was part of Wearwell's.'

Q.2(b): How might other sources of information be used?

'Have works council meetings every two or three weeks and have copies of the discussions typed. A lot of false and exaggerated information is put into circulation every time *anyone* speaks to the management.'

'Monthly meetings.'

'We should receive more information: too much is left to our own initiative.'

'A note about "what's happening" should be placed by management in the weekly pay packet.'

'Management should take more interest in the workers' views.'

'It seems to me that the firm's policy is that the less information you get of any kind, the better the firm likes it, as any information only causes discussions among the workers.'

Q.3(c): What kind of information is required?

'I should like to see a comparison sheet of every firm in the Group. This would be a monthly sheet showing either (a) those units running at a loss or (b) those units showing a profit. It would give the employee an incentive to work hard for his or her employer so that the mill showing the largest profit received a special yearly bonus. Naturally the grade of the worker's cloth would hold the whip hand.'

'Not enough about Wearwell's itself.'

'About my job and any alterations that could improve it, as I think it could be made easier.'

'As a night-worker, I feel we are cut off from the rest of the mill. We feel more could be done to help us by special communication.'

'All subjects. We have to rely on other workmates for technical information, yet if anyone we asked wanted to withhold it he could (some do) so that he has greater security in his job.'

'Much, *much* more about the Group and the mills.'

'The firm could be bankrupt for all we know.'

MILL G

SUPERVISORS AND SPECIALISTS (24)

Q.1. Categories of information

(a) Does the range of information received by supervisors in your mill and described in the statement you have just read

	%
surprise you?	15
confirm your previous views?	80
have no interest for you?	0

Five per cent of the replies were either ambivalent or spoilt papers.

(b) Do you consider the relative percentage of each category of information satisfactory or not? Give reasons.

	%
Yes	38
No	32
Other views	30

See additional comments, p. 80.

(c) Have you any comments to make on the amount of information received by supervisors at the other mill in the research project?

The supervisors, in most cases, offered a quantitative assessment, since only six had any practical knowledge of the other mill.

	%
None	78
Other views	22

Q.2. Sources of information

(a) Does the breakdown of the sources of information in your mill

	%
surprise you?	20
confirm your previous views?	70
have no interest for you?	0
Other views	10

(b) Have you any comments to make on the sources of information available to the supervisors in your mill?

	%
No comment	35
More formality in lines of information	55
Other views	10

See additional comments, p. 81.

Q.3. Information retained

Does the amount of information retained by supervisors in your mill

	%
surprise you?	15
confirm your previous views?	85
have no interest for you?	0

Q.4. More information required

(a) The need for more information was expressed by supervisors in your mill. Does this

	%
surprise you?	15
confirm your previous views?	85
have no interest for you?	0

(b) State the type of information, if any, of which you feel you get too much.

	%
None	85
Rumour	10
Other	5

(c) State the type of information, if any, of which you feel you do not get enough.

	%
Satisfied	40
The job	15
Future plans	30
Current changes	15

See additional comments below.

Q.5. Replies from operatives

(a) Do the replies of the employees in your mill

	%
surprise you?	11
confirm your previous views?	85
have no interest for you?	3
Other or ambivalent replies	1

(b) Have you any comments to make on their replies?

	%
None	85
Surprised at the small quantity of information they receive	15

See additional comments below.

Additional comments

Q.1(b): Is the amount of information in each category satisfactory?

'Departments don't work together.'

'More information on the personnel side would be helpful.'

'The percentage of technical information received seems satisfactory, but information from director–manager level seems lamentable.'

'Fairly satisfactory, although more information regarding personnel matters would be welcome.'

'Personnel information is crazy – a person may be sacked at one mill in the Group and he may be re-employed here!'

Q.2(b): Have you any comments to make on the sources of information available to the supervisors in your mill?

'Supervisors should be notified officially of contemplated changes instead of learning about them from the shop floor – as a result of the grapevine – often from the operatives.'

'I would like to see more meetings between management and supervisors.'

'Suggest that supervisors of departments should be brought together more often to air their opinions.'

'More information could be passed on by more use of our notice board – and the board should be placed in a more convenient and prominent position.'

'Short meetings between management and supervisors would be welcome.'

'If more information was given to all supervisors regarding changes that are about to be made in their respective departments, the people's morale would be even better than it is at present.'

'Not enough information is recorded – all too casual and by word of mouth.'

Q.4(c): State the type of information, if any, of which you feel you do not get enough.

'Need more up-to-date information on takeovers. In other words, what they are likely to mean to our mill – to our jobs. I suggest the publication of a monthly news-sheet covering all Group activities.'

'Need more information about equipment changes.'

'On the whole things work well here. Perhaps more information is needed about union agreements and alterations to methods.'

'In my opinion, supervisors cannot get too much information on any subject, technical, personnel, or financial.'

'I'd like to know about promotions within the Group.'

'I get too much criticism.'

'I get too much indirect information: rumours and guess-work.'

'I am satisfied with the information I get but I was talking to Mr X in another part of the Group and he said that he tried to contact a person responsible for a job only to find that he'd left months ago and that he'd not been replaced.'

Q.5(b): Have you any comments to make on their [the operatives'] replies?

'People don't read notices because the board is too near the clocking-in clocks.'

'I'm surprised that the employees only get two items of information each day.'

'Notice board should be more readily used.'

OPERATIVES (50)

Q.1. Categories of information

(a) Does the amount of information received by your fellow-operatives in your mill, and described in the statement you have just read

	%
surprise you?	15
confirm your previous views?	85
have no interest for you?	0

(b) Do you consider the amount of information in each category satisfactory or not? Give reasons.

	%
Yes	30
No	40
Did not reply	30

(c) Have you any comments to make on the amount of information received by employees at the other mill in the research project?

The 60 per cent who replied to this question gave answers which could only be a quantitative comparison and were too varied to categorize. It was noted, however, by most respondents that the employees in the 'other' mill got more personnel information than was recorded for themselves.

See additional comments, p. 84.

Q.2. Sources of information

(a) Nearly 70 per cent of the information received is by word of mouth from supervisors and your other workmates. Does this figure

	%
surprise you?	10
confirm your previous views?	90
have no interest for you?	0

(b) Have you any comments to make on how other sources of information might be used to help you in your work?

No comment   40%

Typical of the remainder of the replies was a desire for more formality in information; and for notice boards, job cards, training, and meetings.

See additional comments below.

Q.3. More information required

(a) The need for more information was expressed by employees in your mill. Does this

	%
surprise you?	10
confirm your previous views?	75
have no interest for you?	15

(b) State the type of information, if any, of which you feel you get too much.

	%
Adequate	20
None	67
Gossip	10
Other	3

(c) State the type of information, if any, of which you feel you do not get enough.

	%
None	27
General policy and plans	51
Technical and jobs	22

See additional comments below.

Additional comments

Q.1: Amount and categories of information, and comments about other mill.

'Information has *always* been available here: no problems on that score. I suppose it's because we all know the rules and we help each other.'

'Technical information on the whole is as much as an efficient operative can absorb, but information on planning and/or personnel is not forthcoming unless there is a bust-up between us and them.'

'Information regarding my work is most satisfactory but personnel information could be improved. Most of the information we do get is by word of mouth and is usually unreliable.'

'It looks like the *other* mill should have joined MI5 with the amount of information put on the notice board. Maybe it's just to cover a crack in the wall.'

Q.2(b): How might other sources of information be used?

'Personnel matters should be more widely publicized on notice boards. Things are generally quite good here.'

'More information on just why a job is urgent.'

'A few people chosen out of each department should meet with the bosses and information should be passed on.'

'Employees should be allowed five minutes to read the notices on a special-type notice board. This would ensure that everyone got an accurate and regular account of what was happening.'

'As an employee of twenty years' service I am, at short notice, asked to take over as temporary supervisor. My experience is mostly technical, and I have seldom, if ever, been told or shown the administrative side of the job. For example, a sample order for headquarters is checked and passed as satisfactory, but delayed in delivery because I don't know which person has ordered the piece. I have, on several occasions, been embarrassed because I have tried to do my job as best as I can, only to be "told off" for not getting it dispatched. When I give my reason for the delay, I am told, "There is nothing to the job, it will come to you, in time!" In mine?'

Q.3(c): What kind of information is required?

'This poses a problem in as much as the people who pass you information are supervisors who are not equal to the responsibility entrusted to them.'

'It is good here. *Perhaps* more information on working methods.'

'One should never complain of too much information: I take every opportunity to get hold of information and I find the general distribution OK.'

'More information about Wearwell Group – but I must say there is no crisis for lack of news.'

'I'd like more information about the progress of Wearwell's and their expansion scheme. I have read a booklet issued to shareholders and enjoyed reading about the progress being made by different departments in our mill and the expansion scheme carried out by our firm. Not being shareholders, I and my workmates were surprised at what went on behind the scenes to enable us to keep full employment and keep the markets they fought so hard to get years ago.'

ASSESSMENT OF THE RESULTS

The open-ended questions which asked for comments and evaluations produced the most indicative replies but they are, of course, difficult to summarize. Certain conclusions, however, can be drawn from the questionnaire responses as a whole.

SUPERVISORS AND SPECIALISTS

Few people in this group were surprised at the high rate of technical information that was communicated: 86 per cent in Mill F and 80 per cent in Mill G had their previous views confirmed. Many regarded the relative percentages of the different categories of information as satisfactory, though one-third of the participants at Mill G were dissatisfied with them.

There was virtually no comment in either mill on the distribution of the different types of information in the other mill.

The replies to the question on the sources of information were almost identical in the two mills. Most supervisors and specialists recognized that it was unsatisfactory to rely on casual information and they suggested that items should be distributed more formally. They gave specific examples of management's failure to systematize its information and they, like the operatives, left one with the unavoidable conclusion that rumour was too prominent in the dissemination of information.

More supervisors and specialists in Mill G than in Mill F were surprised at the amount of information retained.

Some supervisors and specialists in Mill F were not interested in some of the topics raised by the questionnaires, expressing indifference generally and believing such matters to be of concern only to the management. This attitude was almost completely absent at Mill G.

More information was required and there was hardly any kind of information of which the supervisors felt they received too much. Moreover, the type of information asked for in larger quantities was the type that companies are not usually in the habit of passing on to supervisors: relating to the long-term development of the company, expansion plans, and financial comparisons.

Most supervisors and specialists in both mills knew that the operatives wanted more information. In Mill F, however, nearly one-third in this group were either surprised at, or had no interest in, the operatives' views on the matter.

OPERATIVES

In Mill F, there was a keen interest in Mill G. The operatives would obviously like to have compared their own conditions with those in the other mill, but realized that they were too isolated from it.

Hardly anyone was surprised that so much information came by word of mouth. But it was recognized at both mills that more formality was needed in the passing on of information. It is to the credit of the operatives that they were so clear-minded about how to overcome the lack of formality. In Mill G it was suggested that job cards, notice boards, training, and meetings could help. In Mill F, half the respondents felt that there should be formal meetings with a published feedback, while 10 per cent saw the solution in better supervision.

The answers to the third question were perhaps the most revealing of all. They showed unequivocally that all respondents felt the need for more information. In their answers to the first part of the question, all the operatives in Mill F and three out of four in Mill G felt that the report indicating the need for more information merely confirmed their views. Some of the people in Mill F seemed bitter about the lack of information and most said that it was impossible to have too much information. Several people in both mills commented that they never had any information. In both mills the operatives (as many as 36·3 per cent in Mill F) resented the unreliable gossiping that went on among their workmates. It should be noted that, in Mill G, one in five felt that the amount of information received was satisfactory.

The vital part of this third question was the part that asked the operatives what type of information they felt they should get more of. Except for a small number in Mill F who wanted to know about the financial position of the various units within the Group, the demand fell into two categories: for technical information (50 per cent in Mill F and 22 per cent in Mill G) and for information on the wider aspects of company policy (40 per cent in Mill F and 51 per cent in Mill G).

An important difference between the two mills may be noted here. In Mill G, one out of four respondents said that enough information was being received, but in Mill F there was no such comment.

SUPERVISORS, SPECIALISTS, AND OPERATIVES: SOME
COMMON PATTERNS

1. There was widespread support for more formalized processes
of communication to counteract the inaccuracies of the grapevine, which is a method that thrives when formal channels
either are absent or have broken down.

2. More information was widely felt to be required on a number
of topics, including future policy and the development of the
Group.

MANAGEMENT

This section summarizes, and comments briefly on, the attitudes
of the two mill managers, as expressed in a follow-up interview
with each. Each man had seen the survey results for operatives
and for supervisors and specialists in both mills as well as the
reports on himself and the other manager.

Both managers were surprised at the way information was
circulated from headquarters. Mill Manager F felt that it was
far too casual, adding that he was at the mercy of any Group
executive at headquarters for the provision of accurate information. He considered that communication between headquarters and the old Group of mills had been more efficient.
There was something to be said, he maintained, for passing on
information in a less rigid way, but this did not mean that
Group executives should be excused their responsibility to see
that formal channels worked effectively. He considered that
his own approach to the passing on of information was a
personal one, 'talking to the men as a matter arises'.

One would not wish to challenge the sincerity of the manager
concerned, or his good intentions, but the effectiveness of his
highly commendable personal approach to communication
must depend on (a) the amount of information he receives from
all sources, but particularly from headquarters, and (b) the
way he encourages his immediate subordinates to pass on the

G

information he has given them. The evidence in Chapter 4 and earlier in this chapter suggests that while Mill Manager F 'anticipated' that his immediate subordinates would not retain too high an amount of information they tended to do what *he* did. One supervisor put it this way: 'In dealing with information most of us will be influenced by the way the manager acts and not by what he tells us to do.'

Mill Manager G said that manufacturing and technical communication (that is, messages related to the process) was very good. However, on matters dealing with personnel development and human relations he felt that the flow of information needed improvement. Communication would be so much better if people at the top of the organization presented information to the *right* people. By that he meant that conversation with and comments from senior executives tended to break up the formal presentation of information, and undermined, among other things, status. Meetings between the works director and mill managers were useful and should be more frequent and on a regular basis. Subject-matter should include global issues, that is, matters affecting the overall organization. Also, it would be helpful, he thought, to have information about new methods and research and development. In this respect many mill managers could make a contribution by relating their experience to items of information presented by research and development staff.

Manager G considered that the reason why he received nearly twice as much information as was shown for Manager F was to be found in the normal arrangements of meetings between the works director and mill managers, which stemmed from the old Group of mills. Because there had always been strong links, on a formal basis, between the mills that constituted the 'hard core' of the Group, there was an easy exchange of information between Group executives at headquarters and himself. He took advantage of this relationship by calling into headquarters or ringing up a person rather than engaging in a long-drawn-out correspondence.

The comments of both mill managers revealed a recognition of the value of strong formal links between headquarters and the operational units. Both managers impressed me with their understanding of personnel administration and their concern for proper manpower development. It would seem that Mill Manager G was helped by the closer association of his mill with the original Group as well as by a more effective approach to the process of communication, as reflected not only in what he said (because Mill Manager F also talked of the importance of good communication) but in the way he made decisions too.

This follow-up study may, perhaps, justify the theory put forward by Professor R. Tannenbaum, which demands of the manager that type of behaviour which he would wish to see in his subordinates (Tannenbaum, Weschler & Massarik, 1961).

In other words, outside the autocratic system people will only partially respond to words, and they will normally be affected to a greater extent by their observations of the actions and manner of the leader and of the way he takes trouble to understand his staff.

The size of the operation would not appear to have been a factor in either inhibiting or improving the flow of information in these two mills. No one at any level in Mill F felt that the smaller unit brought any advantage in terms of personnel relations, and, similarly, no one stated that Mill G was at a disadvantage in this respect in comparison with smaller units in the Group.

It would seem, therefore, that while the growth of Wearwell's has created some tension and some uncertainties, these effects are not related to the size of the individual mills. More influential in the communication process were the leadership qualities and behaviour of the mill manager, and, according to the assessment of the managers themselves in the interviews recorded here, the length of time the mill had been associated with the Group.

7

A further study in communication – Mill H

The members of the research team had, since the initial inquiries in the Wearwell Group, been under the strong impression that the flow of information between management and
operatives, and between management at headquarters and
management in the individual units, was more satisfactory in
companies that had a long association with the Group as compared with those that had been more recently acquired. This
impression had not to this point been substantiated by concrete
data, and I therefore felt that a useful purpose would be served
by isolating the factor of association with the Group in one
further study in a mill that had been very recently taken
over.

The research in Mills F and G had fallen into two parts: a
numerical assessment of the amount and types of information
received by three groups of employees; and a follow-up study
which attempted a more subjective analysis of the reactions of
the same groups of people to the state of the communication
system in their mill, as revealed by the earlier investigation,
and which sought, furthermore, to elicit suggestions and opinions
on how improvements could be made.

In this new study I wanted not only to compare the efficiency
of communication in a newly acquired firm with that in the
two mills already studied, but also to deepen the research to a
level where participants' own understanding of what a good
communication system means would be revealed, and, at the
same time, if possible, to assess the priority placed on personnel
matters. To meet these aims, a new questionnaire was drawn

92

up, but in other respects, such as sampling and explanatory meetings, the research methods followed those used in Mills F and G. The introduction of a new type of questionnaire, which, in the event, produced interesting results, meant the sacrifice of a purely numerical comparison between Mills F and G and H. It made no difference, however, to the possibility of an overall comparison.

Mill H was involved in the successful marketing of a new fibre before it amalgamated with the Wearwell Group. It experienced a period of rapid growth and rationalization, which was further stimulated by its merger with Wearwell's in 1964. An early result of this merger was the transfer of some key personnel to Mill H and the concentration there of certain types of production involving a bulked-yarn process.

With such a rapid growth-rate, physical expansion has been continuous since 1960, and major extensions including a dye-house and warehouse have been completed.

At the time of this study, no further large extensions were planned, although a great deal of work was in progress with the object of making the existing buildings, many of which had needed extensive alterations, both more efficient and pleasant to work in. In addition, a new canteen block had been proposed.

The mill is very well sited in respect of accessibility and proximity to potential sources of labour.

The labour force during the period in question was just over a thousand, approximately two-thirds male and one-third female. The majority of employees work in shifts since the plant is operated 168 hours per week. Practically all the labour force is drawn from towns and villages within a five-mile radius of the mill. In addition, some key personnel have been drawn from the Group's other mills, and are now living in the locality. The company employs fairly modern training techniques and has a reasonably well-equipped training school and instructors on the site.

METHOD OF INVESTIGATION

This particular mill met the requirements for this study admirably in that it had been associated with the Wearwell Group for only eighteen months and had not hitherto been extensively canvassed by any member of the research team.

I approached the Group's director of personnel to acquaint him with my ideas for this further study and to obtain his permission, which was readily given, to carry them out. I next spoke to the manager of Mill H, who in the event was most sympathetic to the aims of the research and who later gave me every assistance during its progress.

After department, sex, length of service, and shift had been taken into account, a sample of 10 per cent of works employees was asked to complete a questionnaire. It was felt that this percentage would give a representative sample without producing an unwieldy number of respondents. There were fifteen managerial or administrative staff at the mill and just two (or 13 per cent), one of whom was the mill manager, were asked to complete a questionnaire along with five (about 11 per cent) of the forty-five supervisors, selected at random. Thus there was a responding sample of two members of management, five supervisors, and one hundred operatives. The research that had already taken place and the requirements for the present stage of the project were explained to senior staff at a special meeting. One week later I returned to the mill and checked with the personnel department to discover whether the employees in the sample were at work that day. Those who, for one reason or another, were absent during their normal working hours were replaced by others selected at random so that the final number of respondents was as given above.

The mill manager and the supervisors and specialists completed questionnaires which were handed to me the same morning. (There was one exception, caused by the respondent's having an important visitor; his completed questionnaire was later sent by post.) I then began the task of meeting the one hundred selected operatives. They reported to a rest room, which was being used as an interview room, where they could complete their questionnaires privately and undisturbed. I explained to each one the purpose of the questionnaire and how he or she had come to be selected to complete it; I made it clear that my own position was not one of authority in the company; I also explained the questions themselves and assured the participants not only that their answers would remain confidential and unsigned, but that they would be seen only by me. Although I pointed out, too, that they were in no way obliged to cooperate, not one of them failed to complete the questionnaire.

As stated at the outset, this inquiry was concerned to probe the communication process rather more deeply than the studies in Mills F and G could do, and to attempt an assessment of the priority given to personal development and personnel administration in the company. To overcome the possibility of respondents' selecting the middle of the scale throughout the questionnaire, a number of open-ended questions were included, calling in most cases for subjective definitions. Thus Question 1 asked for a definition of the term 'communication' and Question 2 (a multiple-choice question) for an evaluation of employee relations. Questions 3, 4, and 5 asked whether more information was needed, and, if so, of what kind and from what source (all multiple-choice questions). Question 6 asked for an explanation of the meaning of certain commonly heard phrases such as 'loyalty to the firm' and 'personnel management'. The same questionnaire was used for all three groups of respondents but, in Question 5, the supervisors were asked to ignore the first possible answer and the managers to ignore the first two possibilities.

The questionnaire (which appears as Appendix F) asked for no identifying information and respondents were asked to put their reply in an envelope addressed to me.

ANALYSIS OF THE QUESTIONNAIRE RESPONSES

MANAGEMENT (2)

Although differences were revealed on the more subjective questions, the statements from the two managers were, where definitions were asked for, fairly consistent and precise.

Q.1. Communication means:
'informing subordinates from time to time about company policies, orders, instructions'
'the passing of information from one place to another'.

Q.2. Management–employee relations in the mill are:
'fairly good'
'poor'.

Q.3. More information was required by both managers.

Q.4. The types of information of which more was required related to:
'the Group of companies'
'top executives'
'training facilities'
'promotion'
'what happens to the product after it leaves us and what are its end-uses, so that we could perhaps set more realistic standards'.

Q.5. The information required should come through:
'management'
'company magazine'
'visits to other companies, Group conferences (to get to know what others are doing)'.

Q.6. Interpretation of the following phrases:
Productivity must improve
'more production per operative or per machine in unit time'

'increasing quantity but not at the expense of quality in order to maintain high standards of living'.

Morale in the firm
'attitude of employees towards their job'
'can be bad or good, latter normally associated with progressive companies – humanitarian approach'.

Personnel management
'ensuring that employees are happy at their work and discussing problems with employees'
'specialists within the company, specializing in personnel matters, and in some cases training'.

Labour problems
'shortage of labour, high turnover, unconscientious labour'
'selfish attitudes, lack of understanding in management, restrictive practices, reluctance to accept change'.

Incentive to work
'payment for increased output'
'financial gains, promotion possibilities, opportunities for creative thinking'.

Loyalty to the firm
'willingness to extend oneself for the firm's benefit'
'protecting company interests; doing one's best at one's job'.

Management is interested in the workers
'management thinks about the welfare of the workers and amenities and working conditions'
'good management is interested in the work people and it is responsible for their safety, welfare, and their future'.

It is worth recording here that, prior to the distribution of the questionnaires, I had a personal discussion with the two managers who took part in the study and the senior of the two complained that it was difficult to get hold of certain types of information from headquarters. I asked him if he would specify but he was reluctant to do so. He could only assure me that the kind of information he had in mind would affect the whole

Group of companies but was not of such a nature as to change its competitive position. He added that he normally managed to obtain the information eventually either through the grapevine or from the manager of one of the original mills in the Group.

SUPERVISORS AND SPECIALISTS (5)

The replies from this group indicated a number of misunderstandings as to the meaning of terms and also differences in interpretation between the managers and the supervisors/specialists. In addition, criticism of the company was introduced, not only in answer to questions structured to produce such a response (Q.2), where two of the five supervisors said that employee–management relations were 'poor', but also in the definitions of communication (Q.1). Brief summaries of reactions to a number of phrases (Q.6) are included in the text.

Q.1. Communication means:
'The spirit with which the men work and at the moment I don't think it is very good. But communication will improve once this mill is accepted as part of the Group.'
'Facilities for workers and management to get together, in other words, liaison between the two. It does not happen here.'
'Direct information to foremen and supervisors of various changes made – instead of from other people not responsible.'
'The ease with which ideas and/or intentions can be clearly conveyed by one party to another, without being side-tracked *en route*, and without unnecessary interference or argument by people not qualified to deal with the subject in hand.'
'Getting to know about our promotion. I've heard nothing about my future prospects since the day I joined – some time ago.'

Q.2. Management–employee relations in the mill are:
'poor'
'fairly good'
'fairly good'

'fairly good'
'poor'.

Q.3. More information was required by all respondents.

Q.4. The types of information of which more was required related to:
'promotion' (4 replies)
'training facilities' (3 replies)
'your job in relation to other people's jobs' (2 replies)
'the Group of companies' (1 reply).

Q.5. The information required should come through:
'the mill manager' (3 replies)
'meetings' (2 replies).

Q.6. Interpretation of the following phrases:
Productivity must improve
Of the five replies, two related this term to increased output, two dealt with the quality of the work, and one responded, 'I am at a loss to know how to improve productivity'.

Morale in the firm
All the respondents answered as if they were personally being asked a question and did not attempt to give an overall or objective view. Only one reply was optimistic, 'confidence in the future of the firm', whereas the others said 'unhappy atmosphere', 'rather low because of lack of trust between management and workers', 'moderate', 'could be better'.

Personnel management
There was some uncertainty here, with a range of answers including 'consultants – not managers or producers', 'jobs for the boys', and 'department responsible for settling an employee in a job'.

Labour problems
Criticisms emerged of practices of the 'outside company' (one specifically mentioned Wearwell by name); 'not very

99

good here – too many men leaving to go to other employment'; 'they shouldn't exist but they do'; 'shortage of
labour in some departments causing people to be trans-
ferred to different departments'; 'understandable couldn't-
care-less attitudes because of the outside company'.

Incentive to work

Apart from two respondents who replied 'more pay', there
seemed to be a good deal of confusion as to the meaning of
this phrase.

Loyalty to the firm

There were some thoughtful replies: 'a refusal to believe in
wild rumours and a belief that the firm is working for the
betterment of itself and employed personnel'; 'trying to do
a good day's work, under any circumstances if need be';
'cannot begin to be loyal without proper regard and understanding of the supervisor's job'.

Management is interested in the workers

All respondents distinguished between local and Group
management in their answers and all, except one, felt that
Group management was not interested in the workers. One
supervisor commented: 'We try to be interested in understanding their difficulties but there isn't much example
from what I gather from the outside world (Wearwell
Group) to us.' There was an appreciation of the difficulties
met by the mill management in running the establishment,
but two supervisors felt that management was not interested in the workers, and in one case it was said, 'they
couldn't be, because of the Group changes and policies'.

OPERATIVES (100)

Q.1. The meaning of the term 'communication'.

The meaning of communication was given in the majority of
replies in an abstract way, but was related to the way people
were informed inside the mill. As a result, the following
breakdown of the answers is possible:

Seventy operatives (70 per cent) replied to the question in a personal way and, of these, 85 per cent considered that there were breakdowns and distortions in the system of getting and giving information and that there was need for improvement. Typical of this view was: 'I understand communication to be bad here. The outside management do not talk it over with our men – then our men just put instructions up on the board, and that is what you have to do. I suppose they don't know the reasons themselves. Still, things might improve once we're in the swing of things.' Another 10 per cent considered communication to be good and said that it did not raise problems for them personally although they were aware that other people felt differently. The remaining 5 per cent did not commit themselves but offered examples which amounted to a criticism of the process of communication within the mill.

Twenty operatives (20 per cent) gave a general answer to the question. Examples are: 'communication is to cooperate with each other and to pass on all the relevant information from management to employees'; 'communication is to do with personal development'; 'to create a more humane understanding'.

Five per cent of the replies consisted of admissions of ignorance of the term 'communication'.

The remaining 5 per cent were entirely abusive about communication, without specifying whether their views referred to Wearwell's, the mill, or other jobs they had had.

Q.2. Management–employee relations in the mill are:

	%
Poor	32
Fairly good	62
Good	5
Very good	1
Excellent	–

The conclusions to be drawn from these percentages are obvious. Virtually the entire sample considers relations between the two sides to be less than good – or 'average'. This response becomes even more significant when one recalls that the natural tendency of respondents with regard to 'scale' questions is to support the middle of the scale. One in three, in this case, was in no doubt at all that relations were poor, and aimed for the bottom of the scale.

Q.3. More information was required by all except three operatives who were satisfied with the amount they received.

Q.4. The types of information of which more was required:
(Note: the respondents were able to opt for more than one area of information, and percentages given are of the total number of respondents.)

	%
Promotion	45
Your job in relation to other people's jobs	10
The Group of companies	30
Training facilities	10
Any other information, which included subjects like 'what's to be done in the future?'	5

The information required fell into two main areas: those concerning promotion and the Group of companies. It may seem strange, in view of the criticism of management–employee relations expressed in answers to previous questions, that employees should be so interested in getting promotion in the firm or, indeed, in staying on at all. It also seems rather odd that so many people wanted to know more about the Group of companies, but not one person was curious to know about top executives.

Q.5. The information required should come through:

	%
Your supervisor	15
The mill manager	10

	%
The notice board	5
A company magazine	30
Meetings	35
Other sources	5

Certain deductions may be made from the high support (from a total of 65 per cent of the respondents) for a company magazine and meetings when these responses are related to the replies to the next question.

Q.6. Interpretation of the following phrases:

Productivity must improve

There was a good deal of uncertainty in the replies. This was reflected in the widely differing interpretations of the term 'productivity'. Among the 75 per cent who defined or implied a definition of productivity in their answers, there was very little agreement as to the meaning: 'productivity is about increasing the volume of work . . .'; 'productivity enables us to get better quality without really hindering quantity'. Productivity concerns: 'outside management', 'work', 'the boss', 'the rest of the group', 'the government', 'an American method of work'.

Nevertheless, there was one discernible common thread in the replies and that was that the term 'productivity must improve' involves an external authority making demands of operatives. Thus, 'productivity must improve' means:

'outside management wants us here to work harder'
'the bosses don't care what they ask of us'
'the rest of the Group are relying on us to pull them through'
'the government keeps on about this'
'the government is trying to do better'
'an American method of work which we don't know about and don't need; no one's told us about it anyway'.

103

Morale in the firm

The term 'morale' was defined variously and sometimes even ludicrously. Ninety per cent of the respondents replied as if they were being asked about morale in the Group (55 per cent) or the mill (35 per cent). Only 10 per cent attempted a general explanation of the term. These replies included: 'the means of checking whether people are happy or not in their job and surroundings'. Those who discussed morale in terms of the Wearwell Group or their own mill felt that the 'atmosphere', 'mood', or 'relationships between us all' were 'bad', 'poor', or 'in need of improvement'.

Personnel management

It would seem that only a small section of the respondents knew what the specialist service of personnel management was or attempted to do. However, these people, almost without exception, considered it to be good. In 80 per cent of the replies there was no real indication that the operative knew much about personnel management in the mill, the Group, or elsewhere. These are typical replies arising from uncertainty or ignorance:

'the people who look after our personnel offices'
'a gimmick – so you have to do what you're told; it hasn't changed the company attitude – since Cromwell's day'
'to help management's problems'

or from more fundamental misunderstanding:

'appointed by the government – and just interested in what they can get out of you'
'middle of the road management'
'I can't say what they do – but they seem to do it well'.

Labour problems

The explanations given of this term can be roughly grouped as follows:

%

Shortage of labour means loss of output or breakdown in production   15

Specific instances: absenteeism, management failure   20

Wages should be as in other grades of work or other industries   20

Suggested solutions (a number of references to overcoming 'labour problems' such as 'getting together', 'a bit of give and take on both sides')   20

Why labour problems arise: bad communications (also included in this group are other unclassifiable answers)   25

Incentive to work

The replies centred on the different reasons that people have for working, and are probably the most revealing of all the answers. There was an overlap of subjects in only a small number of cases (ten operatives). All respondents knew what this term meant:

%

Bonus ('the need for a clear bonus scheme', 'more pay', etc.)   35

Happy relationships ('we're not all robots', 'I value peace of mind at work', etc.)   35

Working conditions ('can affect people's ability', etc.)   20

Money and working conditions (a double listing)   5

Happy relationships and money (a double listing)   5

Loyalty to the firm

Sixty per cent regarded the mill as 'the firm', and, of these, one-third thought that loyalty was not possible because of poor industrial relations, bad communications, etc. Forty per cent regarded the Wearwell Group as 'the firm', and all except one of these respondents thought that loyalty was not possible because of poor industrial relations, bad communications, etc.

It would seem that: (a) there is uncertainty about the term 'the firm'; (b) those who regarded the Wearwell Group as the firm said of loyalty: 'not possible', 'not wanted', 'undesirable', 'for what? – we don't know them'; (c) a relatively small number of people felt that loyalty was not possible in the mill (a third of the 60 per cent replied thus); (d) of those who thought that loyalty was possible, this reply was typical: 'to do your best for your fellow-workers and your boss in the mill'.

Management is interested in the workers

This statement put the question of relationships in its more controversial (or prejudiced) form and the responses were fairly crisp and direct.

Five per cent felt that there was truth in the statement:

'Management take part in the work and try to do their best for the workers.'

The remainder emphatically disagreed with the statement:

'They wouldn't shed a tear even if the Wearwell Group was taken over tomorrow.'

'To the management, we are just numbers. The better we do the job, the less notice is taken. It would be appreciated to get a pat on the back sometimes after a job well done.'

'If so, it is not noticeable in this place, unless they find that there is some upset. Then, and only then, do we find that management have any time to know who we are apart from being a clock number.'

'Getting tied up with the outside firm has just about finished any interest that might have been there.'

'Nobody seems to know who the management are, so if we don't know who they are, they don't know who we are and how can you be interested in people you don't know?'

'Only interested in production.'

'Sometimes – when things are going right for them.'

ASSESSMENT OF THE RESULTS

There is a straightforward approach on the part of the management at Mill H towards the question of communication and a recognition of where information should come from if the flow is to be improved. The wider grouping of the units has created a need for knowledge about them which, it was suggested, a company magazine and visits to the other parts of the Group might fulfil, or the existing links between headquarters could be made to work better. The managers' responses to Question 6 showed nothing unusual in, for instance, defining loyalty as 'willingness to extend oneself for the firm's benefit', or in associating labour problems with 'selfish attitudes, lack of understanding in management, restrictive practices, reluctance to accept change'. These might almost be regarded as stock interpretations.

The replies of the supervisors and specialists began to show more differences of interpretation. Understandably, the comments made were specific and less general. Communication was not simply the passing on of information but concerned a particular issue: promotion, training, one's job in relation to others. According to all this group relations between management and operatives were less than good, but the respondents differed as to how they should be better informed.

There were various interpretations of terms like productivity: two said it was increased output; another two, better quality; yet another confessed himself uncertain how to improve it (whatever 'it' was). The personnel function was not clearly understood by the supervisors and specialists. On the question of labour problems, supervisors gave shortage of staff as a contributory factor, a view shared by management. Supervisors looked upon the rest of the companies in the Group with suspicion and consistently referred to them as 'the outside company'. The crispness of management's replies regarding 'pay' as an incentive to work was not reflected in the supervisors' responses to this question. This may suggest that supervisors, being midway between management and operatives, appreciate management's view of pay as an important incentive to work, but are unable or unwilling to ignore the operatives' broader views of incentives, which centre more on satisfaction in the job. The supervisors' replies distinguish between local and Group management and they appear concerned about actions that arise from decisions taken outside the mill; they do not have the advantage, however modest, that the mill managers have, of direct access to headquarters staff.

The operatives' replies confirmed the views of the other groups on the need for improving communication. Operatives also used the phrase 'they' for the Wearwell Group, while the local supervisors and management were 'us'.

The operatives' definitions of the phrases in Question 6 were as interesting for their lack of understanding as for anything else. For instance, it is not to be wondered at that constant encouragement to improve productivity yields disappointing results when some operatives apparently associate the term with 'the boss' or 'the government', or 'an American method of work'.

Answers to the question on morale gave the impression that, while there were no illusions that morale was very good in the mill, it was considered to be a lot better there than in the rest of the Group.

On the question of incentives it was quite clear that good pay, good conditions, and personal relationships were what operatives regarded as incentives to work. In their ideas on this subject, in fact, they were closer to the managers than to the supervisors who, on the whole, gave muddled and vague replies to this question.

The answers on loyalty and interest again demonstrated the distinction made by respondents between the mill and 'the firm' (that is, the Group).

The conclusions to be drawn from this study are:

1. To a much greater extent than in Mills F and G, the supervisor/specialist and operative groups spoke in terms of two levels of organization: 'them' (the outer Group of companies) and 'us' (the mill). Yet there was no obvious support or loyalty for the mill itself, which suggests a confusion arising from the amalgamation of the small unit and a large impersonal one, which then decided policy and practice. Employees no doubt felt that it was pointless to retain loyalty for a unit which had changed so drastically, and it was still more difficult to feel loyalty to the parent Group which had caused these changes. At all levels, employees felt suspicious of and even aggressive towards the Group.

2. This observation suggests that the climate for an improvement in communication would come about only when the mill was accepted as an integrated member of the Group. It does support, in turn, the hypothesis stated at the beginning of this chapter that the length of a unit's association with the original Group of companies is relevant to the state of morale and communication in that unit. In Chapter 6 we saw how Mill Manager G felt that he was assisted in his communication function by the close association his mill had with the original Wearwell Group. Mill Manager F, on the other hand, felt that his mill was not yet on the Wearwell 'grapevine'. The manager at Mill H – an even more recent addition to the Group – felt the same lack of company-wide information as the manager at Mill F. I shall return to the implications of this conclusion in the final chapter.

3. Few respondents below management level had more than a vague idea of the personnel function, a trend noticed in Mills F and G but more pronounced here. In view of the fact that the Group of companies now had a senior executive designated 'Director of Personnel' it would be impossible not to draw the conclusion that there had been a failure of communication both on his part and on the part of the then deputy managing director. The latter had issued a detailed job description for the post (see Chapter 5), but there was no evidence to show that he had reinforced his original announcement with any further company-wide statement on the personnel director's functions. By the time of the inquiry in Mill H, the director of personnel had been in office for more than nine months, but neither he nor the managing director of the division of which Mill H was a part had succeeded in explaining the personnel function even to Mill Manager H, who showed limited appreciation of the term 'personnel management' in his reply to the questionnaire.

4. There was a good deal of uncertainty about the meaning of common industrial terms. This could obviously cause misunderstanding and anxiety, if not downright inefficiency.

8

Research into action: management–staff panels

After the various inquiries described in the preceding chapters were completed, it was felt that the research needed to be given a practical turn. The evidence assembled indicated that management and staff at all levels throughout the units studied felt communication could be improved, and formal meetings were widely recommended as a suitable means of effecting this improvement. The managing director informed me that he did not object to formal meetings but that he would not wish them to be executive or decision-making committees. His view was supported by his immediate subordinate executives who generally felt that 'there is a healthy suspicion of committees in Wearwell's'.

My findings also encouraged me to use formal meetings as the vehicle for action research, but in planning them I decided not to provide them with long detailed agenda or to base their composition on a particular level of authority. It was felt that this type of structure could be considered by participants at the meetings at a later stage. The meetings were not to have any executive authority: to have allowed them this would have involved an entirely new concept in our working relationships, such as exists in countries like Yugoslavia and Israel where worker control is practised. The research unit's aims were more modest and it was agreed that the meetings should have an advisory role.[1] A change in nomenclature emphasized, in a

[1] Rensis Likert (1961, p. 235) has described the need to respect the operating characteristics and performance qualities of the different forms of organization.

fairly simple way, this advisory character: I used the term 'panel' rather than 'committee'.

METHOD

I prepared a brief statement advising the following steps for establishing the panels, and this was given nominal approval by the managing director.

1. (a) *Initial meeting.* A meeting of mill managers throughout the Group will take place to discuss the establishment of panels on matters such as personnel administration, training requirements, welfare trends, etc. It is intended that mill managers will be able to opt for particular subjects according to their interests.

    (b) *Frequency of meetings.* The panels will meet as often as the members require but not less than four times a year.

    (c) *Composition.* A balance between the different levels of authority and the different functions performed will be aimed at, in the composition of the panels. Directors and supervisors will be included, but the nucleus of those attending will be drawn from the middle-management level where the need for improving communication seems greatest. In all, some fourteen people will be invited to serve on each panel.

    (d) *Chairman.* The chairmanship of the panels will be informal. A different person will act as chairman at each meeting unless a particular panel decides otherwise.

    (e) *The servicing of the panels.* The responsibility for preparing any documents required by the panels will rest with the director of personnel, who may wish to use the specialized skills of the research team.

    (f) *Timing.* The panel meeting will last no more than one and a half hours and there will be no set agenda apart from the topic for which the meeting has been convened.

At a meeting on 28 February 1966, representatives of the company and the research team examined this outline and, though they accepted the principles of the communication system put forward, certain alterations were made. The new procedure was set out as follows:

2. (a) Mr Moonman will determine the composition of a panel so that it represents the entire structure of Wearwell (i.e. numerical representation of divisions and specialist functions).

(b) A letter of invitation from the director of personnel will go out to each divisional managing director drawing his attention to the Group managing director's support for the panels and arranging for Mr Moonman or a senior research colleague to call on him individually.

(c) The visit (mentioned in (b)) will enable the research worker to explain to each managing director the purpose of the panels and to ask him to nominate several members of his staff (irrespective of level of authority) who could make a contribution to a discussion on a number of subjects in the personnel field, and who would as well meet certain other requirements referred to elsewhere.

(d) The research team will prepare a list of suitable persons from those nominated to serve on the panels.

It was suggested by the Group managing director that the research team should limit its endeavours to one panel to begin with, and that it should meet at a different venue each time. The members could then tour the premises, and get to know more about the Group and its constituent companies. It should be noted that in this statement the initiative for taking action was placed pretty firmly with the research team. This is not to say that the Group role was ignored. After all, the Group had the ultimate authority as to what was done. It is self-evident that decisions relating to the 'action' process must have the Group's approval and encouragement.

The original proposal for an initial meeting of mill managers had been dropped by this stage in favour of a panel selected by the research team from nominations by the managing directors. I had felt it useful to involve the mill managers fully in the enterprise, but because the managing director and his co-directors considered that this was not the level at which to 'broaden the basis of communication, and because it would mean much planning to bring together all the managers', the alternative approach was accepted. In short, the managing directors of the divisions became the focal point of the project and personal contact with them was to be established.

The informal character of the meetings as suggested by the original proposals was endorsed by the meeting on 28 February. Similarly, the suggestion that the research team should provide briefs for discussion was approved.

The importance of personal contact in the research was appreciated by both the Group managing director and the research team, hence the decision that the director of personnel should write explaining the panels to the divisional managing directors. The complexity of the task ahead was not minimized, but it was felt that a personal visit from myself or a member of the research team to each of the divisions would be more effective than a written request for nominations for the panels. These visits involved journeys to centres at extreme ends of the country. We took the opportunity on the visits to explain to the divisional directors the background to the research since many of the units were isolated from headquarters and because previous inquiries had suggested that they were not always in touch with decisions taken at headquarters.

The target was to establish one panel in the first instance. Because of the interest and the comments of management, it was decided that the panel should concern itself with the education, training, and development of management and staff. However, the intention was to run a second panel just as soon as the structure and procedure of the first had been established. I decided that we should invite up to four nominations for the panels from each managing director. In a division such as filament-weaving, which employed a large proportion of the work force, four nominations would be accepted, but in the smaller divisions – say, merchanting – no more than two names would go forward to the panel list. When all the nominations were in they would be compiled into a register. Only fourteen names were required for the first panel, so it would be necessary for the research team to meet to decide its actual composition, bearing in mind the requirements mentioned under 2(c) and two further criteria which had been approved by the meeting on 28 February. They were: 'promotability' – which meant members of staff who were considered by management to be worthy of further promotion and to be likely to benefit from such a gathering of executives representing different parts of the Group's undertakings; and 'interest in communication' – that is, whether the individual had shown any interest in the general question of communication and in ways of improving it.

The visits to the managing directors were arranged within the fortnight following the February meeting. A letter was sent from the director of personnel explaining the intentions of the project and this was followed by a telephone call from his assistant to all the directors concerned inviting them to suggest dates and times at which the researcher could call. The visits proved satisfactory and in no case did the directors put any difficulties in the way of the research team. The names of executives, supervisors, and specialists were then given to the research worker according to: (a) the contribution they could make to the subject; (b) their suitability for promotion within the firm; and (c) evidence of their interest in the process of communication. By widening the criteria according to which staff would be selected to serve on the panels it was felt that we were engaging in a positive management–staff development exercise in its own right.

In practically all cases the four people who had been nominated were seen and interviewed by a research worker. A final list of names was prepared by the research team and a formal invitation was sent by the director of personnel to those who would form the first panel, along with a questionnaire (Appendix G(i)) and a note suggesting that hotel arrangements should be made if it was likely to prove necessary for the panel member to stay overnight. In addition, a copy of the letter was sent to each managing director so that he would be aware of this latest development.

THE PRE-MEETING QUESTIONNAIRE

The questionnaire was intended to show the level of interest in and understanding of communication matters by those selected for the panel as well as to provide a check on the meeting and on impressions recorded afterwards on a further questionnaire (Appendix G(ii)).

Q.1. What do you consider the term 'communication' to be about?

Communication was regarded by five of the fourteen respondents as a matter involving the organization and concerning the way instructions were given and received. The other nine respondents saw communication in purely personal terms: they required more communication (and therefore more information) on individual promotion and individual claims for training; and they referred to the value of a management development programme or some such scheme.

Q.2. Management–employee relations

Only two of the members of the panel thought that management–employee relations were good. The majority considered them only fairly good or even poor. These responses confirm the general impression gathered from the research hitherto. The majority of the fourteen people in this study had not been involved with the research team before; they had not been interviewed nor had they completed any earlier questionnaires. One corroborative piece of evidence was noted: the more recently a company had joined the Group, the sharper the criticism of headquarters and of company information.

Q.3 and Q.4. Amount and type of information desired

All the respondents required more information under some of the headings specified. Of the topics about which more information was required, 'the Group of companies' came high (given by ten members of the panel), as did 'promotion' and 'training facilities' (twelve references each); also important were 'your particular job' (five references) and 'top executives' (three references).

Q.5. Weaknesses of management–staff panels

Seven replies to the question on what was thought to be the greatest weakness of the panels as a means of improving communication pleaded that to give any answer was difficult or impossible. Fears that there would be no *practical* consequences were expressed eight times (e.g. findings would not be broadcast, grievances would only be aired and nothing would be done about them, the meetings would be devoted merely to the absorbing of information). Some feared that members would be inhibited from speaking frankly. The following reply suggests several important potential sources of failure:

> '... the idea will probably fail if members feel that they are merely being humoured. It could fail, too, if the meetings are so wide in their composition as to have no unity of purpose. They will be less effective than they might otherwise be if top management within the divisions do not understand and support the idea.'

Q.6. Advantages of the panels

Eleven respondents thought the panels useful devices for

bringing personnel from different parts of the Group into closer contact with each other and for encouraging the exchange of ideas. The opportunity they gave for airing grievances was mentioned four times. Help in training and the ability to spread knowledge about broad questions, such as company policy, were mentioned three times each. The initiation of improvements was mentioned twice. Other advantages envisaged as a result of the meetings included the broadening of experience and the facility with which information would be passed upwards, downwards, and across the company structure.

THE MEETING

The minutes of the first panel meeting (see Appendix H) were prepared by an assistant to the personnel director and were eventually sent to all participants and their divisional managing directors. The chairman at this meeting was the director of personnel; all those invited attended, except one manager who was absent on leave. The research team was represented by myself and one other member.

The minutes are a fair record of the panel meeting. Their limitation is that they do not show the mood or behaviour of the individual members or their ability to work together as a group. As the other research workers and I had previously agreed to provide some degree of structure in this first panel meeting, we explained to the participants the background to the project and summarized the sources of disquiet made apparent by the research studies and the completed questionnaires.

Some panel members took the opportunity to 'clear their minds' about personal opinions, but this was not felt to be a negative exercise. It was to be expected from a group of people meeting for the first time in a novel situation. In addition to achieving an understanding of common Group problems, the panel member was put in a position to discriminate between the comments made and to assess the problems and the experiences of others. He was able to relate the importance of all these things to his own circumstances.

THE POST-MEETING QUESTIONNAIRE

The thirteen members of the panel who attended the meeting were subsequently asked to complete a further questionnaire (Appendix G(ii)) which attempted to discover how, as a result of the meeting, they had come to regard communication in the Group. Moreover, did they think that such panel meetings could help to solve communication problems?

Q.1. Need for more information

Eleven of the thirteen members felt that, as a result of the discussion at the panel meeting, it was obvious that there was a need for more information about the Group of companies. Examples given included the following:

'The panel meeting brought me in touch with people I would not normally meet; yet they also, like me, wanted more information about our growth, etc.'

'Staff require information concerning the future development of their particular division, to give them a feeling of security, and to let them know they have opportunity for advancement, together with the development of their particular company.'

'Staff need to have knowledge of training facilities which may be available to them.'

'I knew that communication was far from good but to hear from other people in other parts of the Group that they thought the same was amazing.'

Q.2. Topics on which information was required

Of the topics on which information was required, 'promotion' was given by twelve of the panel members, 'individual jobs' by four members, 'the Group of companies' (e.g. the relationship of one establishment to another) by nine members, and 'training facilities' by thirteen members.

Four subjects were specified separately, as follows:

'Wearwell finished products'

'More information on the thinking motivating the Group'
'Broader knowledge of the activities of the Group, so that
staff have a clearer picture of the part they have to play'
'Technical and production capabilities of each unit'.

Q.3. Advantages of the panels to the participants

In considering the advantages of such meetings to those
participating, over a period of (say) a year, the members
almost unanimously agreed that meeting others from different
parts of the Group and seeing things afresh from their view-
points was an advantage. This reply summed it up: 'The panel
as a whole will, I think, inevitably gain some knowledge of
the activities and problems encountered in other divisions.'
Problem-solving, the fostering of group feeling, and self-
appraisal were the specific benefits anticipated. Some members
thought advantages likely in the realm of training. One, indeed,
thought that the meetings might 'evolve a standard training
scheme for both junior and senior management on management subjects'. Another member saw the initiation of action
as being an important possible result. Such advantages as the
widening of people's 'scale of thinking' and some 'explanation
of Group policy' were also mentioned.

Q.4. Advantages of the panels to the participants' staff

To the first part of this question, which asked whether the
panel meetings were likely to bring any advantages to the staff
of those participating, nine members answered 'yes'. One
replied that he preferred not to comment at that stage and
three gave qualified answers, as follows:

'Not directly due to the participants of the panel but
indirectly if decisions or ideas are taken up by the personnel
department.'

'Only if the views and recommendations of the panel are
implemented at executive level.'

'Yes – with reservations.' (These reservations are perhaps

indicated in this member's reply to the next part of the question: 'this [i.e. in what way there will be any advantages to the staff of members] will depend entirely on the individual panel members and how much they feel they should communicate about the proceedings of the panel.')

To the second part of the question, which asked how these advantages might come about, the following responses were given:

'From action taken by the personnel department, e.g. the creation of training facilities and the dissemination of information.'

'Members will be furnished with information gained from open discussion with other employees that will help each member to be more Group-minded particularly if some of the criticisms are justified and some ideas brought to fruition.'

'(1) Closer cooperation between companies within the Group. (2) Discussions on training facilities that operate in individual companies so that eventually these might be run on a Group basis.'

'The panel will make suggestions for our directors' approval which will ensure that talent, ability, and loyalty are recognized and rewarded, that adequate training facilities for advancement are provided, that the progress of staff is reviewed and reported regularly, and that promotion is seen to be made on acceptable grounds.'

'People on the panel themselves will be going through a development exercise, and their staffs will benefit from working for someone who is better informed and perhaps a little more loyal to the Wearwell Group.'

'The staffs should be able to get a clearer outline of their own prospects.'

'By the mere fact of having listened to problems as they are experienced throughout the Group and having discussed these at some length, one can probably look at training within one's respective unit and broaden the horizon with the obvious long-term benefits that could come the way of trainees.'

'Either by verbal liaison (difficult) or better still by the distribution of a news-sheet covering promotional training schemes, vacancies within the Group, activities and news of a general nature which could be interesting to the staff. Such a news-sheet should appear four to six times a year at least.'

'The panel members can explain to their staff the difficulties other people in other mills have to overcome and what may be best for one mill (us) may not be best for the Group as a whole.'

Q.5. Are there any other matters that you would like to raise?

The replies of the panel members to the final question are given below:

'I felt that in order to give the panel momentum it might have been right to submit a subject on which a sub-panel could prepare a report for discussion at the next meeting.'

'Labour recruitment; a system whereby people working in corresponding positions in the various units have equal rewards; Group research on improving productivity. This may require a small, highly skilled panel.'

'What about communication to the outside world? Most people when told of our company either have not heard of it or think it is a biscuit firm.'

'I think that at future meetings a more specific subject should be put up for discussion, e.g. supervisor training, Group training, newsletters, inter-firm visits, etc.'

'A strict and regular supervision of each unit within the Group to ensure at all times good working conditions, and good standards of conduct and discipline between directors, managers, and staff, to avoid excessive losses in skilled labour.'

'I would suggest that the panel should attempt to categorize the levels of management and staff within the Group who could receive training and then go on to recommend what form this should take. We must be careful not to allow discussion to become too general and informal, waiting to see what turns up.'

'How to attract the right type of person into the textile industry and retain them.'

SOME GENERAL INFERENCES

The conclusion that has already been drawn about the general state of communication within the Group is reinforced here: the meeting and the answers to the questionnaires brought out people's wish for more information than they had previously had. Various statements made both at the meetings and in the questionnaire responses indicated a desire for a more formalized system of communication. Although it was suggested that a new spirit or attitude as regards the interchange of information was needed (e.g. it was stated at the meeting that supervisors were said not to be sufficiently interested and that the board should let information filter down; and the questionnaire replies emphasized that panel members should be willing to pass on information), members clearly felt that this would be insufficient without formal methods of maintaining an adequate information flow.

The answers to the pre-meeting questionnaire showed a significant relationship between the number of references to poor or merely fair communication and the references to lack of information on subjects such as 'promotion' and 'training'. The significance of this is further underlined in the open-ended questions.

In the answers to Question 1, communication was interpreted in personal terms by the majority of respondents. There was a cautious response to the panel meetings; fear that there would be no practical consequences was specifically mentioned (Question 5).

The replies to the post-meeting questionnaire endorsed the need for more information and for those types of information mentioned in the pre-meeting questionnaire. The fears as to the value of the panel meetings were overcome in the positive and clear answers to Questions 3, 4, and 5.

Even allowing for the modest number of people involved and for the fact that they had had only one meeting, there was strong support for the idea of a panel of staff of different levels of authority and from different mills as a means of improving communication. Perhaps even more important, one could see the emergence, at this first panel meeting, of specific and common problems on which there had previously been inadequate information and which were felt to be communication problems. Thus difficulties of labour recruitment and promotion were openly discussed and solutions were suggested. The implications of this approach will be examined more exactly in the concluding chapter.

The main reason for ignoring the conventional committee meeting structure at a particular level of authority was to encourage greater participation and, at the same time, to involve, as far as possible, representatives of the Group as a whole. In the arranging of the meeting and the assessment of its success, two factors were taken into account:

authority anxiety – a formal committee meeting can prevent a free flow of discussion when different levels of authority are represented, and it was hoped that the panel structure would avoid this;

degree of involvement – whether the meeting would enable those attending to make a contribution in a way that showed their concern and interest in the subject under discussion.

On both these counts, the panels appeared to be successful. In terms of *authority anxiety*, the panels appeared to reduce the autocratic and formal atmosphere usually associated with meetings of people at different levels of authority. This was shown even after the first meeting by the answers to Questionnaire G(ii) and by the frank criticism of the growing Group of companies expressed by men who might naturally be expected to have some uneasiness as to the affect of their words on their own positions.

The value of a discussion meeting correctly conducted is that it is likely to lead to a much higher *degree of involvement*. The comments of the executives in the headquarters study and during the initial inquiries indicated that they wished to be involved in what was going on: to give and receive information and to 'feel part' of the company on matters in which they were particularly interested. The replies to the questionnaire and the comments at the panel meeting would suggest tentatively that it was the type of activity the panels offered that was required. The answers to the post-meeting questionnaire, in particular, tend to support Professor McGregor's thesis, referred to earlier, that there is a close correlation between the way people are encouraged to participate in setting themselves goals for improved performance and the achievement of these goals. An increase in participation on the part of the individual member of staff also tends to produce improvements in his relationship with the Group as a whole.

Apart from the panel members themselves feeling involved to a much greater extent in company matters, it was felt that participants at future panel meetings could play a useful role in supplying feedback to their divisions. Soon after a panel meeting the divisional managing director could discuss its proceedings with those who had attended it and with other appropriate staff, and, in particular, any proposed action relevant to that division. The panel members could also decide what would be the best method of keeping their divisions informed, whether, for instance, by further meetings within the division or by some other means. The panels would therefore provide psychological participation for a great many employees.

It was not assumed that the panel meetings would run themselves. Such a technique of cooperation and communication, it was supposed, would demand increasing support from the participants as well as proper planning and continuous servicing from the secretariat, which was to be provided by the personnel department.

9

Conclusions and recommendations

The Wearwell Group has grown into an organization of such vast proportions that the vital process of communication, it is suggested, must cease to depend merely on the unplanned activity of individuals, however well-meaning and enlightened. The process of passing on information must be efficient. This chapter will summarize not only the aims of the investigation but also the experiments carried out. In addition, certain practical policies will be suggested which, in view of the facts obtained from the research set out in preceding chapters, seem appropriate to the problems of the Wearwell Group and to companies of comparable size or rate of growth. There is, of course, no blueprint for success in this field: personal attitudes often prove incalculable; a formal system of communication once established must, as a primary aim of management, be maintained enthusiastically.

In the introduction, attention was drawn to the theories on which a total study of the subject of communication could be based. I decided that a purely mechanistic approach, as exemplified by Joseph Pelej's definition of the process of communication, 'Management must communicate through systems and procedures',[1] would not suffice. I considered it necessary to add to the systems and procedures two other elements of communication: individual influences (the personality factor), and social influences (group cohesion). I preferred to see communication as a process of human activity. As

[1] Pelej, J., International Systems Meeting (Conference), Los Angeles, October 1957.

R. A. Stogdill (1959) put it: 'Communication between any two members may be regarded as a kind of interaction and as a kind of performance.'

The aims of an inquiry must be limited to the resources available. In the Wearwell project, it was necessary to concentrate on one aspect of the total organization. Hence my study was concerned with three mills and Group headquarters. Apart from the more usual methods of investigation, action research was also implemented in an attempt to test and assess solutions suggested by the research.

I was able to complete the action research, despite constant organizational changes, an inevitable condition of working within a dynamic organization. Relationships between the research team and company staff were always friendly, even, after a time, 'matey'.

It became apparent soon after the beginning of our investigation that there was a somewhat casual approach to organizational responsibilities both in the mills and at headquarters. In the personnel field, all candidates for a job at one mill were interviewed by the mill manager and, as we saw, he would supplement his interview by driving near to a man's home to assess the state of the place. While there may be an advantage in such an individual approach to personnel management there was here – and in other cases – no record or system to back it up.

Contrary to popular industrial mythology, not all staff think highly of a casual structure of authority and responsibility. Indeed, in our investigations we found little or no support for the casual or spontaneous forms of control that were evident in certain parts of the Group. On the whole, respondents seemed to be asking for more formality in much the same way that the research team had required to know the exact role of everyone, whether from the university or the Wearwell Group, who was concerned with the project. Neither mill operatives nor research workers can tolerate for too long an overtly casual approach to authority, and thereby decision-making, in a changing situation. A Group Services Board had been set up in Wearwell's before the research was initiated, in order to deal with the coordination of various operations and to provide a specialist function in personnel, for instance, but, for the reasons stated above, this was not a success.

The intensive study of the two mills, F and G (Chapter 4), showed that very little information was being distributed to operatives. One of the findings was that at both mills about two-thirds of the operatives would have liked to receive more information, principally about the Group of companies. Indeed, the desire for more information of a general nature was not confined to operatives. It was concluded that at Mill F most supervisors felt that more information about the firm ought to reach them in a more formal manner. Only a few held that point of view at Mill G so it was significant that general information comprised some 26 per cent of the total information received by supervisors at that mill, compared with only 12 per cent at Mill F, where the supervisors felt discontented. For the managers, it was shown that one of the advantages they derived from attending a works managers' meeting was that it proved to be a fruitful source of new information about the firm. It was also indicated that, for managers, information about organizational matters was supplied by unspecified grapevine sources and through newspapers. Operatives clearly required more information on the wider aspects of company policy. Moreover, the type of information supervisors wanted to receive more frequently and in greater detail was of a nature that companies are not usually in the habit of passing on to supervisors: relating to matters such as the long-term development of the company, expansion plans, and financial comparisons.

All these findings constitute a strong case for keeping employees at all levels better informed about the wider aspects of Group policy and progress. A number of proposals as to what steps might be taken, as interim measures, to meet the demand for information were included in Chapter 4. However, at the follow-up in these mills just two months later, there were sharper criticisms about the ways in which information was being dealt with and decisions were being taken (Chapter 6). The method of inquiry on the occasion of this follow-up was somewhat unusual: questionnaires elicited responses to a summary of the answers that had been given by the same respondents during the earlier study.

It was obvious that, during the two intervening months, feelings had intensified; as a result they were expressed more forcibly. At the operative level, all the operatives in Mill F and 75 per cent of those in Mill G said that the generally felt need for more information confirmed their own view on the matter. Some of the operatives seemed positively angry about the lack of information: 'The firm could be bankrupt for all we know.' The summary of the operatives' replies to the questionnaire used in the original study was shown to a group of supervisors and specialists. In Mill F, it was noticeable that a number of supervisors expressed no interest in their operatives' views on the lack of information. A number of supervisors went so far as to regard the operatives' remarks contemptuously: 'Those who are critical don't stay too long in Wearwell's.' Perhaps a more significant remark by a supervisor (and an indication of why operatives felt the lack of information) explaining why he did not pass on information was: 'Ninety per cent of the information I get has no bearing on what I'm doing.' Whether this comment indicated a genuine failure by management to provide the 'right', i.e. appropriate, information (according to the supervisor), or a failure on the part of the supervisor to appreciate the operatives' interest in what, to him, seemed irrelevant material, requires further study, but even so I hazard some suggestions later.

Both mill managers showed themselves sensitive to their responsibility to transmit information within their own mills. They thought that some of the criticisms made by the supervisors and operatives during the follow-up ought more correctly to be directed at headquarters for not having established a formal method of communication with the mills. Part of the improvement, noted earlier, in the flow of information in Mill

G would seem to derive from that mill's close association with the old Wearwell Group, a view also expressed by the manager. He said, 'There is a casual – not a formal or regular – exchange of information between me and the Group executives.' Nevertheless, fortuitous personal contact is hardly a substitute for an organized system of recognized responsibilities and authority among different levels of staff.

Two other experiments were conducted, whose results amplify these preliminary conclusions. One took place before the follow-up study in Mills F and G (Chapter 5: Investigation at head office), the other at a later stage in the project (Chapter 7: A further study in communication – Mill H). The aim of the head-office investigation was to assess the flow of information among executives themselves and between the executives and the mills. Fifty-one interviews were conducted over a period of a month. A most important feature of this study – as in the research in Mills F and G – was the opportunity we were given to follow through the effects of the circulation of inconsistent information. For instance, a great deal of positive support for the idea of a management conference was squandered by the unsatisfactory way in which staff were allowed to learn about it. At different times during the month, executives reported to me that 'a conference was to take place'. The message had been received by them according to no order of seniority or level of responsibility. An even more significant example of breakdown occurred over the publication of a report of an earlier management conference.

The disquiet expressed on both these matters was quite considerable. Conferences that bring together management and staff from a Group of companies are without doubt a desirable activity, but much goodwill can be lost by the inability of the decision-makers to plan effectively the actual announcements and subsequent reports-back.

Clearly, the criticism of certain executives that they did not know of the conference until 'everyone else knew' is partly a reflection of the lack of a clear structure in the organization.

It might at the same time be argued that if you have managers of the highest calibre they will obtain for themselves all the information that is relevant to their work and responsibility. However, that is to ignore the long-service average executive who maintains a competent but not outstanding performance. To get the most out of such people, a strong organizational structure is required to ensure that they experience no uncertainty about their duties and roles in a changing environment.

It became apparent during the research that the term 'communication' was being used as an 'umbrella' phrase for complaints against conditions which could not be said to be part of the communication process. The importance of understanding the utility nature of the term 'communication' in this study cannot be over-stressed. Because it is a fairly familiar term used by management and trade unions, it tends to be misapplied, with the result that questions of management development, training, staff turnover, and payment systems may be ignored. An effective and accurate method of communication is, of course, necessary, but its value must be seen in perspective. In a similar way it is, unfortunately, easy to generalize about other expressions and phrases, such as 'loyalty (or lack of it) to the firm'. We have seen in Mill H and elsewhere some of the difficulties employees experienced in identifying themselves with 'the firm'. A detailed examination of the particular subject of loyalty in Wearwell's, which amplifies this point, has been made by J. G. Foster (1966): 'Loyalty to the firm is really loyalty to the firm as it appears to the individual and this appearance or image depends on the firm's policy . . .'

Foster also discovered in his study of mills in the Wearwell Group that there was a correlation between length of service and loyalty to the firm. In one notable case, there was a drop in loyalty to and interest in the firm between the second and fifth years of service. If this loss of loyalty were to cause people to leave, it would mean a substantial addition to the Group's recruitment and training bill. In a number of jobs, employees are able to make a direct contribution to the mill almost immediately; but in others, particularly where younger workers are concerned, it may take a considerable time before their skills are able to justify their training. Clearly, this is an area of inquiry which should be taken up in greater detail than was intended by Foster in his investigation. He says, very aptly: 'If a firm is sure that it wishes its employees to feel loyal to it for any reason, it has in its own power the ability to encourage and maintain their loyalty.'

At this point I should like to consider whether there is any significant difference in the efficiency of the communication process between a mill with a long association with the Wear-well Group, like Mill G, and one only recently associated with it, like Mill H. There can be little doubt that the study in Mill H revealed that communications were less good there than in any other single unit studied. Yet it should be recognized that, with the passage of time, the closer association of people with one another is likely to improve personal understanding and thus communication. Nevertheless, it is necessary both to identify the causes of breakdowns in communication and to improve the working relationships of staff with each other at the earliest possible stage in the taking over or merging of companies. The research here has emphasized: (a) the need to provide the manager with information that is relevant to his immediate and long-term duties, and (b) the importance of recognizing the elements of distortion that operate in the passing of information between different levels of authority. For example, the term 'productivity' evidently presented no difficulty to the managers when they were asked to explain it. Yet it had been so inexpertly explained to operatives that almost without exception they defined it pejoratively, associating it with 'the government' or with 'an American method of work'.

The studies in Mills F, G, and H suggest that a communication system can work on a casual basis but that its success may depend to a large extent on the proximity of the mill to the Group – not physical proximity but proximity in mental attitudes, the closeness of men who are known to each other and have built up an understanding over a period of years.

The evidence from executives, managers, supervisors, and operatives suggests that improvements in communication would help working relationships within the Group. G. Stockdale (1966) puts it this way:

> It could be argued that merely because a person says 'takeovers cause a reduction in personal contact' does not mean that this issue is important ... but if several hundreds of individuals, without hesitation or persuasion, repeat the sentence, then surely the issue must be important to these people as a body.

The implications of our investigation and subsequent argument are in line with the thesis presented in *The dock worker* (Liverpool University, 1954), which is that changes in the structure of an industrial community (or indeed of any society) do little to improve social relationships unless they are in harmony with the purposes and attitudes of the individuals involved. In a splendid commentary the authors say: 'Those who initiate such [organizational] changes must exercise a responsible concern for the needs and feelings of the individual men and women whose ideas and ways of life will inevitably be affected.' In action research, we take this counsel a stage further and suggest some of the tools management might use to ensure that the employees play a constructive part when technical and operational changes are introduced.

We had reached the point in our investigation when it was desirable to introduce, with the cooperation of the managing director, some technique that would improve communication. The research findings indicated that the meeting would be an acceptable technique to use: it could help to foster a feeling of belonging to the one Group, and discussion of policies and practices throughout the Group might help to overcome some of the difficulties experienced in individual units. The often-expressed need for a greater range of established procedures in communication can frequently be satisfied by a system in which the meeting of employees plays a central part. It was recommended that a system of meetings should be established and carefully maintained.

Perhaps the most important characteristic of meetings of the kind described here is that they cut across the various existing levels of authority and responsibility. The pilot meeting that took place did not consist entirely of directors and supervisors, but of directors, managers, supervisors, and specialist staff, all as equal members, representing each of the divisions. There are obvious advantages, in terms of increased mutual under-standing, in a meeting between various levels of authority, which need not be dwelt on again. The report of the meeting and replies to the subsequent questionnaire (Chapter 8) re-vealed a strong, pervasive feeling, noted elsewhere, that employer–employee relations in the Group were not good enough and that meetings whose membership did not corre-spond with the formal organizational structure would help to improve them. It was felt also that the meetings could facilitate the flow of information: there would be less danger of various items of information fossilizing at one level of authority. Additionally, such meetings would be a useful source of up-ward communication. In other words, they would keep management in touch with what was happening at other levels in the organization.

It should be emphasized that the meetings of the proposed panels were to have no executive power. Their function would be purely advisory. They would be concerned with imparting, discussing, and feeding back information. Decisions could not be taken but communication needs could be aired and fully discussed. Participants would be able to gain an insight into wider Group problems and would be expected to pass these impressions on to their colleagues and to report to the meeting on reactions to them. But they would not be concerned with the exercise of constitutional power. It was hoped that a side-effect of such meetings would be the development of the participants themselves: they would have their experience widened by the very fact of taking part, and training might be a prominent item on the agenda of the meetings. But this training function would have to remain incidental, and efforts would have to be made to keep it so. It would not be desirable for these meetings to be regarded as a practical exercise indulged in by an ambitious and favoured few. Rather, they should be seen as a valuable contribution to the everyday management of the Group.

There was one further weakness in the organization of the Wearwell Group that the research tended to underline – that was the need for a clear and defined direction in personnel and staff development. Although a senior personnel appointment had been made by the Group, the manner of the announcement and the 'lost' job description of the personnel director suggest that another attempt would have to be made to centralize this work and to establish it on a more authoritative footing so that personnel management and development of staff would have a fair chance of success. The original appointment was less successful than it should have been for the reason stated, but also because it was known that the executive chosen to fill the post, a first-rate textile manager with a good deal of common sense and friendliness, was not a personnel specialist in a situation that was becoming increasingly complex.

A top-line specialist should supervise the running of the communication system between headquarters and the individual units. He should be based at Group headquarters, not only because, as an officer serving the whole Group, this would be the appropriate place for him, but also because, during the research, the view was often expressed that headquarters was remote and that senior management did not take an interest in the lower grades or did not pass on enough information. In other words, one of the principal tasks in communication ought to be done at headquarters. The officer's duties should be concerned mainly with the development and appraisal of staff so that the major item of concern, namely 'information about us and them', would be adequately dealt with on the level of the individual's performance and development. He should prepare the agenda and minutes of the suggested meetings, and generally act as secretary of such meetings. His staff should prepare organization charts and keep them up-to-date. It could be argued that these functions could equally well be discharged by the existing personnel department. However, it became increasingly obvious that the existing personnel function was not being covered imaginatively so that it is conceivable that the new officer would take control of the whole personnel function. The personnel department had been unable to prevent a deterioration in communication in the past so it is unlikely that, as at present organized, it could support the formal system that is suggested in this chapter.

However, it should not be felt by other managers that, merely because there is a specialist in communication and personnel development in the Group, they are absolved from giving advice and on-the-job management training to their subordinates. It has been stated previously that communication is one of the more important activities of management. It is to be hoped that whatever management training opportunities exist in the Group will be brought to the attention of more people as a result of the implementation of the various proposals in this chapter and that the proposals will lead to closer thinking in the Group on the significance and nature of sound management.

The first proposal was for a system of meetings that would promote the interaction of people at all levels in the Group; the second advocated, as a means of improving the structure, the creation of a central personnel authority.

A third and final proposal concerns the need to avoid discrepancies in basic information such as emerged at various stages in our inquiries. The introduction of a handbook was suggested earlier (Chapter 4) and by Foster (1966) in his thesis.

Such a handbook would have to be specifically designed for the Group: taking account of the continued rapid expansion of Wearwell's, it should recognize the individuality of each unit in the Group, while at the same time showing how it fits into the wider organization. Thus growth should be seen as a natural development – not as a series of imposed fits and starts. The functional work of the specialists as well as the responsibilities of management and supervisors, for example, should be explained and supplemented from time to time.

The handbook could be presented in two parts, covering the following topics:

Part I A general survey of the textile industry
    (a) Developments leading to the present state of the industry
    (b) Factors influencing the development of the industry on a large scale and the relationship between the different operations
    (c) The world-wide markets (with tables on the main producing countries and areas of increasing demand)
    (d) Control of the industry in Britain and the changing pattern of control

Part II The Wearwell Group and its growth
    (a) History of the company
    (b) Description of the divisions
    (c) General policy of the Group
    (d) Organization – for action.

I examined many examples of Group handbooks in an effort to find one that might be adapted for use in the Wearwell Group, but I found almost all of them unsatisfactory. Either they were written in language that the average employee would not understand, or they were sophisticated prestige journals. A good example of a handbook issued by an expanding company is that used on supervisory training courses by United Steel Companies Limited. This company utilizes the book as part of a training exercise. No handbook should be handed over to an employee unless an opportunity is provided for the employee to discuss its contents with his superior. So, ideally, a handbook should be distributed by management and supervision. Not only can this procedure have a positive effect on the personal relationships between management/supervision and operatives, but it can lend support to the authority of the manager/supervisor, who is at the same time fulfilling his role of communicator.

Clear diagrammatic presentations can often be of more help than explanatory prose. The United Steel Companies' handbook (1963), for instance, includes a map showing the location of units and a graph illustrating output.

The interim lines of action put forward in Chapter 4 seem still to be relevant at the end of the investigation. The value of the panel meetings will need to be gauged according to the consequences of their work in the different divisions and on different subjects. While this process continues it is necessary for something to be done at once to improve the quality of personal relationships in the mills and the organization as a whole and, for this end, the proposed managerial–supervisory meetings (see p. 41) should be made an obligation in each unit. The best way of ensuring accuracy of subject-matter is, as a preliminary step, to have regular meetings between Group executives and specialists at headquarters. It may be that if these major and supporting proposals were properly handled, it would not be necessary to look beyond them for the necessary improvement.

On the wider national aspects of the subject of attitudes in an expanding organization, I would make a plea for a central register on research in this and related behavioural fields to be maintained by a government department.

There is no common problem of communication that affects all the units of this expanding Group of companies. The seriousness of breakdowns in information would seem to depend on a number of variables, including the length of the particular mill's association with the main body of the Wearwell Group and the attitude of the unit manager towards his job and particularly to that part of it that concerns human relationships. The manager is thoroughly involved in human problems whether he likes it or not. The social consequences of his work are therefore an integral part of his profession.

Headquarters staff also have problems of communication. Whereas many people in the mills felt that staff at headquarters were privileged and 'in on things', this was not found to be the case. Uncertainty – sometimes anxiety – about the development of company policy was expressed even by executives at Group level.

In conclusion, I would put forward certain lines of further inquiry that are suggested by the present research:

1. There are now two types of meeting operating within the Group of companies: those meetings run on authoritarian principles (managerial–supervisory) as well as the democratically structured panel meetings introduced during the course of the present research. A comparison of their effectiveness could be made. In addition, an inquiry could be undertaken into the way the two forms of meeting are interlocking and integrating with the communication flow within the Group.

2. It is not possible to make an authoritative assessment of the advantages and disadvantages of the methods used in this research. This would require comparable material acquired by other methods under similar conditions. The present investigation could, however, be the basis of future work. In particular, the daily record of information received and disseminated, which was used in Mills F and G, could be extended to a number of other mills.

3. The closer integration of many of the technical processes used in the Group has now started and will, no doubt, affect the way in which higher management decisions are made.

The links between the divisions, mills, and headquarters are, at the moment, somewhat tenuous and could be strengthened by such operational changes. Whether or not this is the case would be an interesting field of research.

4. Further study is required into the reasons for behavioural differences between executives, because, until some of them have been identified, efforts to make existing managers more effective are likely to meet with limited success. In this connection, it should be recorded that several months after the fieldwork of the present research had been completed, the managing director of the Group left. As Winifred Raphael (1948) noted in a monograph, changes at higher management level have an enormous influence throughout an organization, affecting work practices and interpersonal relations. A research worker would be ideally placed to pursue this concept.

Within the limitations of this inquiry, action research would appear to merit serious consideration as a means of following through a specific piece of research and of testing proposals arising from it. Management and employees at all levels saw the research worker not as a consultant or as an investigator but as a specialist making a contribution to their own knowledge of what was taking place in the firm and pointing the way to improvements. Slightly sceptical and uncertain at first, individuals soon found that the opportunity to express their views freely to an impartial listener gave them immediate satisfaction and relief. They realized that the confidence that they gave was being used without bias to enable their views to be expressed upwards in a way quite new to them. But these studies did more than that: they are early attempts to measure the strengths and weaknesses of the current systems of communication. Conclusions can at present be only of the most tentative kind, but they already indicate the need for new thinking. Further surveys are required before sound generalizations can be advanced.

Appendix A

BRITISH INSTITUTE OF MANAGEMENT

MANAGEMENT RESEARCH: NOTES FOR GUIDANCE

The amount of data collection and social research being carried out in offices and factories is increasing. It may be expected to increase still further during the next decade to provide industry-wide committees and other bodies with up-to-date relevant information. It should also enable social science teachers to make further contributions to management education. But since there is seldom complete identity of interest between the social research worker and operating management, it is important that the basis for any cooperation be more fully understood. This is particularly essential in the early stages of negotiation when the areas of research inquiry are being defined. Each needs a sufficient appreciation of the other's purposes and of the character and structure of the organizations in which each works. For example, the social research worker is concerned with contributing to new knowledge and will generally expect to publish the results of his research whereas operating management will be inclined towards gaining information to improve the profitability of the business.

As a starting point, it may be helpful to suggest that the conditions for study of any part of a business organization are likely to be essentially similar to those put forward by a research or academic body in permitting access to itself for similar purposes to an outside person. For research studies cannot prosper when the enterprise sees itself, however unwittingly, as the victim rather than partner in the study, nor if the research worker believes he is being steered away by management from asking appropriate questions.

Appendix A

The initiative to carry out research into management comes mainly from two sources –

(a) the research worker requesting permission to enter an enterprise to test hypotheses and pursue certain ideas of his own, or
(b) the enterprise inviting a research worker into its organization to look into a specific problem.

Whatever the basis of their relationship, both the research worker and the enterprise will benefit by making explicit certain points concerning academic freedom on the one hand and the enterprise's relationship with its staff, its suppliers, customers, and competitors on the other.

The following propositions, based on experience, are designed to clarify that understanding and so facilitate the growth of social research on mutually acceptable lines:

1. At the stage of exploratory contact between representatives of a business firm and a social research group, the methods of working and conditions of publication should be discussed. Such agreement needs to be explicit. It could take various forms according to circumstances. When drawing it up, the points which follow should be considered.

2. The enterprise, on agreeing to any research that involves discussions with its staff or access to the company's papers, should insist on the right to see all the research findings before publication. This can, with advantage, be done for three reasons –

(a) to remove any errors of fact, and, on the other hand, to clarify any differences of opinion or interpretation;
(b) to consider any implications in the report which might affect the reputation of the enterprise or the research group;
(c) to ensure that anonymity and/or confidentiality is adequate and in agreed terms.

3. Suitable arrangements for anonymity will be agreed with the enterprise unless their written permission is given to the contrary.

4. In matters of principle arising out of any report and affecting its public position, the enterprise must have the right to withhold consent to publication of the whole or part. In such cases, it should however communicate its position to the relevant persons in the University or College concerned, with a view to pinpointing the areas of disagreement.

5. In cases where the difference of opinion is one of interpretation of the facts, the research worker will be under an obligation to include at the end of his article, and indeed as part of it, any observations that the enterprise wishes to make.

6. The enterprise, on agreeing to research of any kind being carried out, should nominate a senior person to whom the research worker is responsible for advice, planning, and making contacts, etc. This senior person, either personally or through a representative, will undertake to introduce the research worker to the heads of all departments likely to be affected by the study or survey. This is to ensure that the significance of the work and what is involved is accepted and agreed by them.

7. The research worker before publication – which includes using data in seminars and lectures – is under an obligation to show all his facts and figures to the official(s) nominated by the enterprise.

8. Wherever practicable the research worker will arrange to present working papers or interim reports to the official(s) of the enterprise before completion of the survey.

February 1965

Appendix B

UNDERSTANDING AND APPRECIATION OF THE RESEARCH WORK

Initial interviews

A chart, in a brief form, of my impressions of the reactions of the executives whom I interviewed

Executive / Manager	Scale	Brief comment
A	II	Hazy
B	III	To help the company in a way
C	I	Does not know what the point is, does not care
D	III	A joint project between industry and the academic world
E	IV	Can specify research theory and names of workers
F	II	Not very clear
G	I	Does not understand
H	III	The university has been brought in to put out the fire
I	I	Does not understand
J	II	Consultants have been brought in
K	IV	Names and research mentioned
L	III	Understands research and its value to the company
M	I	Does not understand
N	II	Part of an O & M study from the college
O	IV	Can specify the intentions of the research project
P	I	Does not understand
Q	II	Hazy
R	II	Consultants are now extending their work to attitude survey

METHOD

During the course of the interview, a series of questions was put to management on: (a) the names of the research workers; (b) the aims and purpose of the research work; (c) the relationship between the company and the university; (d) the problems associated with the company's development and organization and what might be done to put them right; (e) the long- and short-term aims of the company.

Their answers were related to the following scale:

I *Did not understand.* Did not know names of research workers and was not able to refer to any aspect of the project.

II *Partial understanding.* Not able to state names but could say that the university was doing something (very hazy reference to subject, how it originated, etc.).

III *Understanding.* Aware of the company's link with the university. Could specify an area likely to be dealt with in research.

IV *Understanding (in detail).* Could specify two or three areas of research. Could refer to other important research projects.

V *Understanding (appreciation).* Able to assess the value of the research. Knew the names of the research team. Aware of the company's needs and problems.

Appendix C

QUESTIONNAIRE P2 (1)
OPERATIVES

These questions are concerned with the information which you may have received about the firm, the mill, your job, or yourself, and with the events of the last working day.

Please complete the questionnaire as quickly as possible by placing a tick or number in the box as requested.

1. Have you received any items of information about your job or the firm in the last day?

    YES ☐   NO ☐

2. How many? ☐

3. How many items of information did you receive on the following subjects?

    Technical matters   ☐
    Personnel matters   ☐
    General problems and plans ☐

4. How many did you receive in the following ways?

    By notice board   ☐
    By word of mouth   ☐
    By personal written statement ☐
    Other   ☐

5. How many did you receive from the following sources?

    A workmate   ☐
    A supervisor   ☐
    The manager   ☐
    The trade unions ☐
    Other   ☐

Mills F and G   *Strictly confidential*

QUESTIONNAIRE P2 (2)
SPECIALISTS/SUPERVISORS

These questions are concerned with the information which you may have received about the firm, the mill, your job, or yourself, and with the events of the last working day.

Please complete the questionnaire as quickly as possible by placing a tick or number in the box as requested.

1. How many items of information did you receive about your job or the firm in the last working day?   ☐

2. How many items of information did you receive on the following subjects?

   Technical matters   ☐

   Personnel matters   ☐

   General problems and plans   ☐

3. How many items of information did you receive from the following sources?

   Mill manager   ☐

   A work colleague   ☐

   Other   ☐

4. How many of the items of information which you received within the last working day had to be

   Retained   ☐

                                          state number
                                          in each case

   Passed on to someone else   ☐

Mills F and G   *Strictly confidential*

QUESTIONNAIRE P2 (3)

MILL MANAGER

These questions are concerned with the information which you may have received about the firm, the mill, the job, or yourself, and with the events of the last working day.

Please complete the questionnaire as quickly as possible by placing a tick or number in the box as requested.

1. How many items of information did you receive about your job or the firm in the last working day? ☐

2. How many items of information did you receive on the following subjects?

   Technical matters   ☐
   Personnel matters   ☐
   General problems and plans   ☐

3. How many items of information did you receive from the following sources?

   Other mill managers   ☐
   Head office   ☐
   Mill staff   ☐
   The trade unions   ☐
   Other   ☐

4. How many of the items of information which you received within the last working day had to be

   Retained   ☐

                                        state number
                                        in each case

   Passed on to someone else   ☐

INTERVIEW CHECKLIST
Questions used to stimulate discussion

OPERATIVES: Do you receive as much information as you would like?

Is the information you receive of the right sort?

SUPERVISORS: (Since completing yesterday's questionnaire...)

Has anyone asked you a question which you were not able to answer about the job, your department, the mill, or the Wearwell Group?

Did you consider such a question important and do you think you will be able to find out the answer?

Have you learnt anything entirely new about the firm recently?

Have you attended any meetings?

Did you hear about some of the details concerning your work today before you arrived at the mill?

Is the information you receive of value?

MANAGERS: (Since completing yesterday's questionnaire...)

Has anyone asked you a question which you were not able to answer about the job, your department, the mill, or the Wearwell Group?

Did you consider such a question important and do you think you will be able to find out the answer?

Have you learnt anything entirely new about the firm recently?

Have you attended any meetings?

Did you hear about some of the details concerning your work today before you arrived at the mill?

What sort of contact have you had with Group headquarters? (visitors, 'phone, you visited, letters)

Is the information you receive of value?

Appendix D

Strictly confidential

QUESTIONNAIRE P2 (4)

MANAGEMENT

These questions are concerned with the information which you may have received about the firm, the mills, the job, or yourself, and with the events of the last working week.

1. How many items of information did you *distribute* about your job or the firm on the following subjects in the last working week?

    Technical matters   ☐

    Personnel matters   ☐

    General problems and plans   ☐

2. How many items of information did you *receive* on the following subjects?

    Technical matters   ☐

    Personnel matters   ☐

    General problems and plans   ☐

3. Indicate the amount of information *distributed* to:

    (a) The mills   ☐

    (b) Other departments at headquarters   ☐

    (c) Outside agencies and clients   ☐

    (d) Deputy managing director and board   ☐

4. Indicate the amount of information *received* from:

    (a) The mills   ☐

    (b) Other departments at headquarters   ☐

L   153

(c) Outside agencies and clients ☐

(d) Deputy managing director and board ☐

5. Since completing the last questionnaire has anyone asked you a question or questions which you could not really answer? If YES, was it about:

    (a) Job
    (b) Department
    (c) Mill
    (d) Wearwell Group

Also, state   (i) Was it important?
                (ii) Do you think you will ever be able to find out the answer?

6. Since completing the last questionnaire have you, yourself, asked a question which could not be answered?

    (a) Was it important?
    (b) Was it about:

        (i) Job
        (ii) Department
        (iii) Mill
        (iv) Wearwell Group

7. Did you learn anything entirely new about the firm this week. If YES, please specify.

8. How many calls have you had from mill managers in the last working week?

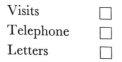

    Visits   ☐
    Telephone   ☐
    Letters   ☐

9. How many meetings have you had in the last working week? Please specify.

Appendix E

STATEMENT OF RESEARCH UNDERTAKEN AT MILL F AND AT MILL G
December 1965 – January 1966

CONCERNING SUPERVISORY STAFF

1. *Categories:* At Mill G, supervisors receive mainly technical information (57 per cent), then general (26·4 per cent), and personnel (16·6 per cent). At Mill F, the distribution is as follows: technical 56 per cent, personnel 31·5 per cent, general 12·5 per cent.

2. *Method:* The principal source of information for both mills is generally colleagues, 47·7 per cent.

3. *Information retained:* At Mill G supervisors retain 59·2 per cent of all information received; at Mill F, 47·5 per cent is retained.

4. *More information required:* The majority of supervisors and specialists would welcome more information presented in a more formal manner.

> *Note:* It must be emphasized that these comments and statistics are merely tentative and in no way are they to be regarded as a final statement on the research work carried out by the University of Manchester research team.

STATEMENT OF RESEARCH UNDERTAKEN AT MILL F AND AT MILL G

December 1965 – January 1966

CONCERNING OPERATIVES

1. *Quantity and quality of information:* Employees at both mills receive an average of 2·1 items of information each day. The information received is considered to be of value.

2. *Categories:* At Mill G, the vast majority of information received is technical (70·3 per cent) while at Mill F information is more evenly divided between technical (42 per cent) and personnel (52 per cent).

3. *Method:* At both mills, information is received mainly by word of mouth (72·6 per cent) from supervisors and colleagues.

4. *Notice board:* The notice board is used more at Mill F than at Mill G (for 11 per cent of items against 6·2 per cent).

5. *More information required:* Most operatives would like more information but are vague about their exact requirements.

Mills F and G

QUESTIONNAIRE P3
OPERATIVES

I. AMOUNT AND CATEGORIES OF INFORMATION

(a) Does the amount of information received by your fellow-operatives in your mill, and described in the statement you have just read

surprise you?	☐
confirm your previous views?	☐
have no interest for you?	☐

(b) Do you consider the amount of information in each category satisfactory or not? Give reasons.

(c) Have you any comments to make on the amount of information received by employees at the other mill in the research project?

2. SOURCES OF INFORMATION

(a) Over 70 per cent of the information received is by word of mouth from supervisors and your other work-mates. Does this figure

surprise you? ☐

confirm your previous views? ☐

have no interest for you? ☐

(b) Have you any comments to make on how other sources of information might be used to help you in your work?

3. MORE INFORMATION REQUIRED

(a) The need for more information was expressed by employees in your mill. Does this

surprise you? ☐

confirm your previous views? ☐

have no interest for you? ☐

(b) State the type of information, if any, of which you feel you get too much.

(c) State the type of information, if any, of which you feel you do not get enough.

Mills F and G

QUESTIONNAIRE P3 (1)
SPECIALISTS/SUPERVISORS

1. CATEGORIES OF INFORMATION

   (a) Does the range of information received by supervisors in your mill and described in the statement you have just read

   surprise you? ☐

   confirm your previous views? ☐

   have no interest for you? ☐

   (b) Do you consider the relative percentage of each category of information satisfactory or not? Give reasons.

   (c) Have you any comments to make on the amount of information received by supervisors at the other mill in the research project?

2. SOURCES OF INFORMATION

   (a) Does the breakdown of the sources of information in your mill

   surprise you? ☐

   confirm your previous views? ☐

   have no interest for you? ☐

   (b) Have you any comments to make on the sources of information available to the supervisors in your mill?

3. INFORMATION RETAINED

   Does the amount of information retained by supervisors in your mill

   surprise you? ☐

   confirm your previous views? ☐

   have no interest for you? ☐

4. MORE INFORMATION REQUIRED

   (a) The need for more information was expressed by supervisors in your mill. Does this

      surprise you? ☐

      confirm your previous views? ☐

      have no interest for you? ☐

   (b) State the type of information, if any, of which you feel you get too much.

   (c) State the type of information, if any, of which you feel you do not get enough.

5. REPLIES FROM OPERATIVES

   (a) Do the replies of the employees in your mill

      surprise you? ☐

      confirm your previous views? ☐

      have no interest for you? ☐

   (b) Have you any comments to make on their replies?

Appendix F

QUESTIONNAIRE P4
SAMPLE OF MANAGERS, SUPERVISORS, AND OPERATIVES

1. There is a lot of talk nowadays both in this and other companies about 'good communication' and 'bad communication'. Please write what *you* consider the term 'communication' to mean. (Use the space provided.)

2. Do you think that management–employee relations here are

Poor	☐
Fairly good	☐
Good	☐
Very good	☐ *tick one of*
Excellent	☐ *the boxes*

3. Would you like more information about your job, or the company?

Yes	☐ *tick one of*
No	☐ *the boxes*

4. If you answered YES to Question 3, please state the type of information of which you would like to have more.

Promotion	☐
Your job in relation to other people's jobs	☐

The Group of companies   □
Top executives   □
Training facilities   □   *tick one or more*
Any other – please specify   □   *of the boxes*

5. If your reply to Question 3 was YES, how would you like to receive this information? Through:

    Your supervisor   □
    The mill manager   □
    The notice board   □
    A company magazine   □
    Meetings – such as a works
        council   □   *tick one or more*
    Any other – please specify   □   *of the boxes*

6. State, in a few words, what is meant by the following phrases:

    Productivity must improve:

    Morale in the firm:

    Personnel management:

    Labour problems:

    Incentive to work:

    Loyalty to the firm:

    Management is interested in the workers:

    When completed, please place this questionnaire in the envelope provided, and return to Mr Moonman.

161

Appendix G(i)

MANAGEMENT–STAFF PANEL
QUESTIONNAIRE

(pre-meeting)

1. There is a lot of talk nowadays both in this and other companies about 'good communication' and 'bad communication'. Please write what you consider the term 'communication' to be about. (Use the space provided.)

2. Do you think that management–employee relations here are

Poor	☐	
Fairly good	☐	
Good	☐	
Very good	☐	*tick one of*
Excellent	☐	*the boxes*

3. Would you like more information about your job, or the company?

Yes	☐	*tick one of*
No	☐	*the boxes*

4. If you answered YES to Question 3, state the type of information of which you would like to get more.

Promotion	☐
Your particular job	☐
The Group of companies	☐

Top executives   ☐

Training facilities   ☐   *tick one or more*

Any other – please specify   ☐   *of the boxes*

5. On your understanding of the management and staff panels, what would you say would be their greatest weakness as a means of improving communication within the Group of companies?

6. What in your opinion are the advantages of having the management and staff panels?

Note: Please return this form by Tuesday, May 24th, to Mr E. Moonman, Department of Management Sciences, University of Manchester, Sackville Street, Manchester 1.

Appendix G(ii)

Confidential

MANAGEMENT–STAFF PANEL
QUESTIONNAIRE

(post-meeting)

1a. Would you say, as a result of the discussions at this panel meeting, that there is a need for more information about the Group of companies.

    Yes   ☐

    No   ☐   *tick one of the boxes*

1b. Now, please give at least *two* examples as to why you answered yes or no.

2. As a result of the discussions at the panel meeting, what would you say are the most important items of information which should be distributed to the staff of Wearwell?

    Promotion   ☐

    Individual jobs   ☐

    The Group of companies   ☐

    Training facilities   ☐   *tick one or more*

    Any other – please specify   ☐   *of the boxes*

3. Now that you have attended the first panel, would you say what you consider the advantages of these meetings are *likely* to be over a period of, say, a year, to those participating.

4a. Do you think that there are likely to be any advantages to

164

the staffs of those participating as a result of the panel meetings?

4b. If you answered Y E S, please show how.

5. Are there any other matters that you would like to raise?

Now, return this within 5 days *to Mr E. Moonman, Department of Management Sciences, University of Manchester.*

Appendix H

MANAGEMENT–STAFF PANEL MEETING

Held at Wearwell headquarters

Subject: Education and Training (Management and Staff)

Present: (a list of those present followed plus an apology for absence)

A detailed statement was given by the research workers on the original aims of the project, the work covered to date, and the range of interviews completed.

Mr Moonman asked the panel to consider the following points:

1. What responsibility has a manager for improving human relations or communications?

2. Can any one company or division or mill run its own staff development scheme?

3. Is poor communication related to a lack of opportunity for the individual?

4. Are complaints alleging poor communication related to the complainant's own success or failure?

Mr Moonman concluded by saying that neither he nor the other research worker would join in the discussion unless it was felt to be absolutely necessary. They would, however, give their comments at the end.

The discussion part of the meeting was opened by various comments about the availability of the right kind of labour, and the methods to be employed to retain labour once it had been recruited.

Mr B said that the old middle-grade of school-leavers was no longer coming into textiles as before but was tending to stay on at school for further education. In his case, he felt wages and prospects were largely to blame (warehousing being regarded as a 'dead-end' job by those people), while Mr F felt that a lot of the trouble stemmed from the problem of wage structure as imposed by the trade unions, which did not allow sufficient flexibility in rewarding individual loyalty and effort.

As an incentive to retaining labour, Mr C quoted his experience of a mill in the United States where every operative was being trained for another job at the same time that he was carrying out his present work. Mr A said that this was possible in some areas but numbers trained must bear a relationship to opportunities available to avoid disillusionment. People must also be trained to improve their performance in their current job.

Mr W added that there was always the need for some people to stay in the lower-paid jobs.

Mr D said that the problem of retaining people in his particular unit was once again money; and he felt that it was important to pay people, particularly those with a family, a wage which would make them comfortable, and more if possible. Further attempts were being made at his mill, he added, to attract and retain labour, by directing their training scheme at the school-leaver. Jobs were being made more attractive and less boring. He quoted the instance of one young worker who had started in the warehouse and was progressing through the laboratory and dyehouse, having had it explained to him that he might quite possibly be a shift supervisor by the time he was 27 or 28. For operatives generally they had attempted to introduce as much automatic machinery as possible in order to cut down on the number of employees and to make the job more interesting and better paid.

Referring to Mr D's comments about training, Mr A wondered whether this could be done simply within X company. Did they not need the facilities within the rest of the Group to help with this? Mr D agreed that a move-around within the Group would be helpful for these people. The approach so far, he added, had tended to be parochial.

Mr J expressed the opinion that if many units in the Group were parochial in their approach to training it was out of necessity rather than design. There were at present insufficient resources to send people out. He felt that training often ended either in disappointment or in the loss of people who had had money spent on them during training; but this was to be expected. Where it was felt that opportunity was lacking, it was due to the individual company and not to Group communication.

Mr E, referring back to some of the comments of his colleague Mr D, said that it was not possible to train a knitter once he was over 29 years of age. The labour force must be caught between the ages of 17 and 29. They had lost twenty men over the past twelve months although they had been able to replace them. People who were recruited were very soon lost to firms who worked only day-shifts. Absenteeism was a particular problem in night-shift work.

From the chair Mr A asked if Company X trained people just for themselves. Mr D replied that this had not been treated as a Group scheme as yet and he met with some agreement from Mr H, who said that each unit was unique and, therefore, tended to look after its own interests. Mr J felt that a timetable for management development would fail. People should be more involved and have opportunities outlined to them. They should not be moved automatically from department to department.

Mr G pointed out the danger of frustration if people were not promoted after having been trained, and wondered whether, when a vacancy was not immediately available, it would not be possible to give the brighter chap some added responsibility in his present job. He added that if this were to happen the person ought to have added authority at the same time and consequently the individual unit could do this on its own but ought to be given more guidance on policy from headquarters.

Asked by Mr W if he felt that operatives wanted to improve themselves, Mr G replied that he thought they did. He had found this the case at his mill recently because of expansion and improved prospects. Mr C agreed on this point and said it would be true where there was expansion. For staff, on the other hand, expansion was not necessary as an incentive because they could be moved from mill to mill in any case.

On the question of change within a unit Mr K commented that there was some worry about the future at his mill with the change from weaving to warp-knitting because operatives did not know all the details. Mr T wondered whether the mill manager himself knew all the details that ought to be passed down. Mr W added that the manager should be given information from board level so that he could assure operatives that their jobs were secure. Future plans and developments should be confided to him more fully.

Mr C suggested the use of a newsletter to keep people informed and added that it need be published only when there was something to say and need not be a regular thing.

Mr L said that at his mill there was no set communication procedure. There were production meetings but they were used simply to talk about production matters. People were not told, for instance, that machinery was due to be moved until it was actually disappearing. He added also that at his mill the trend was single management progression – one man being geared for one job. On the whole question of communication Mr D said that there could be justification for some sort of relations officer to pass on information by word of mouth. Even then, however, some information must be kept back until the last minute. The problem was how much information to release, and when to release it.

Asked by Mr A if he felt managers were given enough opportunity to communicate, Mr N said that he felt they were and that information was passed down. The filter-down of information tended to cease in some cases at the supervisor, however, because not every supervisor was sufficiently interested in the people below him.

On the question of promotion Mr F said that he had known people to leave because of a wrong promotion or because of insufficient opportunity for training and for getting further qualifications. He felt that promotion should be by results. Mr H added that a person who had not been promoted should be told why.

Mr H said that there was much operative training within

his company but opportunities for development within the Group were not known.

Mr A wondered whether it was possible to release people for training – and, if so, whether mill employees were the right people to be given this kind of training. Mr H replied that it was possible to some extent, but that even so a few people had been lost because the opportunities for individual development in the Group were not known.

Mr C felt that facilities within the Group should be available to train people in depth, to give them more idea of all aspects of management. The idea of a Group training scheme met with approval from most members although the problem of people from different units comparing wage-rates was mentioned.

The research workers then gave their views as to how they saw the situation.

The first speaker pointed out the danger of losing the best people if they were not moved about from unit to unit to gain experience. Suggestions as to what the members at the meeting felt should be done should be put to the board. There was the added problem of what information was required and how it should be circulated. The board should be persuaded to let information – reasons for change, growth, policy, etc. – filter down.

In his summing up, Mr Moonman stated that a plan or programme for training and development was important. Young people must first think at mill or unit level, since this was where their first loyalty lay. Furthermore, supervisors must be taught to create good relations with their immediate contacts from the outset.

Commenting on the content of the meeting Mr Moonman said that it was obvious that communication was poor, and not just in one or two units. He again raised the point that people should be told when and why they had not been promoted since people had been known to leave because they did not know why someone else had been promoted in their place.

On the question of how far the individual could be responsible for information outside his own unit, Mr Moonman said that success would depend on people knowing what was going on throughout the Group.

Mr Moonman had noted the concern that had been expressed at the possibility that workers from different mills, brought together as a result of some Group training scheme, might take the opportunity to compare wages. It was something that had to be circumvented. This obstacle should not be allowed to stand in the way of such a scheme; if necessary, rationalization would follow. A Group training scheme, he said, was a necessary innovation.

In conclusion, Mr Moonman suggested that before the next meeting a brief should be prepared to inform members of the panel of the training facilities in the Group and how they were being used.

References

Chapter 1

BURNS, T. & STALKER, G. M. (1961). *The management of innovation.* London: Tavistock Publications.

FENSHAM, P. J. & HOOPER, D. (1964). *The dynamics of a changing technology.* London: Tavistock Publications.

GROSS, BERTRAM (1964). *The managing of organizations.* New York: The Free Press.

HOMANS, G. C. (1950). *The human group.* New York: Harcourt Brace; London: Routledge & Kegan Paul, 1951.

LEWIN, K. (1946). Action research and minority problems. *J. soc. Issues,* **2.**

MCGREGOR, D. (1960). *The human side of enterprise.* New York: McGraw Hill.

The Manager, November, 1965.

MAYO, E. (1933). *The human problems of an industrial civilization.* New York: MacMillan.

MOONMAN, E. (1961). *The manager and the organization.* London: Tavistock Publications.

RICE, A. K. (1958). *Productivity and social organization.* London: Tavistock Publications.

ROETHLISBERGER, F. J. & DICKSON, W. J. (1939). *Management and the worker.* Cambridge, Mass.: Harvard University Press.

SPROTT, W. J. H. (1958). *Human groups.* Harmondsworth: Penguin Books.

TANNENBAUM, R. & SCHMIDT, W. (1958). How to choose a leadership pattern. *Harvard Business Rev.,* **36** (2).

TRIST, E. L. & BAMFORTH, K. W. (1951). Some social and psychological consequences of the longwall method of coalgetting. *Hum. Relat.,* **4,** 3–38.

Chapter 3

WILSON, A. T. M. (1955). A note on the social sanctions of social research. *Sociol. Rev.,* **3** (1).

Chapter 5

CICOUREL, A. V. (1964). *Method and measurement in sociology.* New York: The Free Press.

Chapter 6

TANNENBAUM, R., WESCHLER, I. R. & MASSARIK, F. (1961). *Leadership and organization.* New York: McGraw Hill.

Chapter 8

LIKERT, R. (1961). *New patterns of management.* New York: McGraw Hill.

Chapter 9

FOSTER, J. G. (1966). *Loyalty in an expanding organization.* Manchester: Unpublished M.Sc. Thesis.

LIVERPOOL UNIVERSITY SOCIAL SCIENCE DEPT. (1954). *The dock worker.* Liverpool: Liverpool University Press.

RAPHAEL, W. (1948). *The influence of higher management on the working group.* Manchester: Manchester College of Technology, No. 13.

STOCKDALE, G. (1966). *A study of attitudes in an expanding company.* Manchester: Unpublished M.Sc. Thesis.

STOGDILL, R. A. (1959). *Individual behaviour and group development.* New York: Oxford University Press.

UNITED STEEL COMPANIES LTD. (1963). *Staff training pamphlets* (1). Sheffield.

General Reading

ACTON SOCIETY TRUST (1953). *Size and morale.* Part I. London.
ACTON SOCIETY TRUST (1957). *Size and morale.* Part II. London.
ARGYRIS, C. (1957). *Personality and organization.* New York: Harper.
BARNARD, C. I. (1948). *The functions of the executive.* Cambridge, Mass.: Harvard University Press.
BENDIX, R. (1956). *Work and authority in industry.* New York: Wiley.
CARTWRIGHT, D. (1951). Achieving change in people: some applications of group dynamics theory. *Hum. Relat.*, 4, 381–92.
CARTWRIGHT, D. & ZANDER, A. (Eds.) (1960). *Group dynamics: research and theory.* (2nd edn.) Evanston, Ill.: Row, Peterson; London: Tavistock Publications.
FESTINGER, L. & KATZ, D. (Eds.) (1953). *Research methods in the behavioral sciences.* New York: Holt, Rinehart & Winston.
FOUNDATION FOR RESEARCH ON HUMAN BEHAVIOR (1954). *Leadership patterns and organizational effectiveness.* Ann Arbor, Mich.
FOUNDATION FOR RESEARCH ON HUMAN BEHAVIOR (1959). *Communication in organizations: some new research findings.* Ann Arbor, Mich.
HAIRE, M. (Ed.) (1959). *Modern organization theory.* New York: Wiley.
HARE, P., BORGATTA, E. F. & BALES, R. F. (1955). *Small groups.* New York: Knopf.
VENS, M. (Ed.) (1963). *The practice of industrial communication.* London: Business Publications.
JAQUES, E. (1951). *The changing culture of a factory.* London: Tavistock/Routledge.
JAQUES, E. (1956). *Measurement of responsibility.* London: Tavistock Publications.
KAHN, R. L., MANN, F. C. & SEASHORE, S. E. (Eds.) (1956). Human relations research in large organizations, II. *J. soc. Issues*, 12 (2).
LEWIN, K. (1947). Frontiers in group dynamics. *Hum. Relat.*, 1, 5–41.
LEWIN, K. (1948). *Resolving social conflict.* (Edited by Gertrud Lewin.) New York: Harper.
LEWIN, K. (1951). *Field theory in social science.* (Edited by D. Cartwright.) New York: Harper; London: Tavistock Publications

LEWIN, K. (1958). Group decision and social change. Pp. 197–211 in E. E. Maccoby, T. M. Newcomb, and E. L. Hartley (Eds.), *Readings in social psychology*. (3rd edn.) New York: Holt, Rinehart & Winston.

LIKERT, R. (1958). Measuring organizational performance. *Harvard Business Rev.*, **36** (2), 41–50.

LIKERT, R. (1961). An emerging theory of organization, leadership, and management. In L. Petrullo and B. M. Bass (Eds.), *Leadership and interpersonal behavior*. New York: Holt, Rinehart & Winston.

MCGREGOR, D. (1950). Changing patterns in human relations. *Conference Bd Mgmt Rec.*, **12** (9), 322.

MCGREGOR, D. (1957). An uneasy look at performance appraisal. *Harvard Business Rev.*, **35** (3), 89–94.

REVANS, R. W. (1957). *The analysis of industrial behaviour. Automatic production-change and control*. London: Institution of Production Engineering.

THELEN, H. A. (1954). *Dynamics of groups at work*. Chicago: University of Chicago Press.

Index

absenteeism, 12, 105
action research, 2ff. (definition),
  128, 134
aims of author's inquiry, 3–4, 19,
  29, 30, 141
authority, 6, 10, 18, 21, 50, 54,
  60, 111, 114, 124, 131, 135
authority anxiety, 124–5

background to the study, 13–18
Bamforth, K., Trist, E. L. &, 10
bonus scheme, 105
British Institute of Management,
  3, 20, 143–5 (App.)
Burns, T. & Stalker, G. M., 9, 24

canteen, provision of, 27, 93
'Case of the Unknown Management Conference Report,
  The', 63–8
central register for behavioural
  studies in industry, 139
Cicourel, A. V., 51
committees, 51, 111, 112, 124
communication
  and length of association be-
    tween unit and Group, 25,
    40, 91, 92, 109, 133
  and size of unit, 25, 40, 91
  concept of in industry, 4
  definitions of, 4–5, 11, 96, 98,
    100–1, 116, 132
  formal system of, 39, 127, 128,
    130, 131

informal system of, 39
information on attitudes to,
  21, 22
quality of, 25
see also information
communication between Group
  and University of Man-
  chester, 19, 20, 24n.
company handbook, 41, 137–9
company magazine, 96, 103, 107
company philosophies, 58
comparison sheets, 77
conclusions and recommendations, 41, 127–41
conferences, 58, 62, 96
Contracts of Employment Act
  (1963), 65
control, the nature of, 7
conversation, time spent in, 9
creative participation, 11

depression of 1951, 28
Dickson, W. J., Roethlisberger
  F. J. &, 8
director of personnel and training, 64–6, 94, 110, 113, 114,
  115, 116, 118
see also Executive Q
director of purchasing, 29
discipline, 59, 122
discriminating response, 11
discussion groups, 66
Dock worker, The (Liverpool University), 134

executive, author's definition, 12
executive changes, memos of, 53
executive training courses, 53
Executive: A, 52; B, 53; C, 53–4;
    D, 54; E, 49, 55; F, 55; G,
    56; H, 56; I, 57; J, 58; K, 59;
    L, 60; M, 61; N, 61–2; Q,
    54, 58, 64n.
executives and mill managers,
    contact between, 47

family concerns, 26
family links among personnel, 13
Fensham, P. J. & Hooper, D., 10
filament-weaving division, 17,
    27, 53, 61, 115
Foster, J. G., 132, 133, 137
fringe benefits, 57, 66
further possible lines of research,
    140–1

'good relations', tradition of, 21
grapevine, 46, 53, 81, 89, 98, 109,
    129
Gross, Bertram, 11
group attitude, 46
group cohesion, 127
group dynamics in industry, 7
Group Executive Board, 17, 18
Group management conference,
    47, 50, 63–8
Group Services Board, 6, 17, 18,
    60, 61, 64, 128–9
Group structure, 64–5
growth, *see* rapid growth

handbook, 41, 137–9
head office, investigation at, 42–
    68
    analysis of interviews, 51–68
    analysis of questionnaire re-
        sponses, 43–51

attendance at meetings, 48
'Case of the Unknown Man-
    agement Conference Re-
    port, The', 63–8
inability to answer questions
    put by others, 45–6
inability to obtain answers to
    own questions, 46
learning about the organiza-
    tion, 46-7
methods of communication,
    47–8
recipients of information dis-
    tributed, 44
sources of information re-
    ceived, 45
three main types of informa-
    tion, 42–3
types of information distri-
    buted and received, 43–4
Homans, G. C., 8
Hopper, D., Fensham, P. J. &,
    10

incentives to work, 97, 100, 105,
    108
Industrial Training Act, 65
information
    about Group and its policies,
        35, 36, 39, 41, 43, 44, 49,
        50, 73, 76, 78, 80, 85, 86,
        87, 88, 89, 99, 102, 117, 119,
        129
    about Group finances, 76, 82,
        87, 88
    about individual jobs, 99, 107,
        117, 119
    about promotion, 96, 98, 99,
        102, 107, 117, 119
    about top executives, 117
    about training facilities, 96,
        99, 102, 107, 117, 119, 123

information (*continued*)
about working methods, 86,
    90, 123
by word of mouth, 38, 39, 59,
    74, 81, 85, 87
formal presentation of, 84, 88,
    89, 90, 91, 123
from outside sources, 36, 37,
    38, 41, 73, 75
inconsistent, 131
personnel, 39, 43, 44, 48, 49,
    50, 81, 82, 85, 90
printed, 76
technical, 36, 37, 38, 39, 40,
    43, 44, 48, 49, 50, 73, 76, 78,
    81, 82, 84, 85, 86, 88, 90
written, 38, 59, 76
see also head office, investiga-
    tion at; Mills F and G, first
    and follow-up studies in;
    Mill H, study in
involvement, degree of, 124–5
Israel, 111

job cards, 44, 88
job descriptions, 55, 64–5

labour problems, 97, 99, 104–5,
    107, 108
labour recruitment, 14, 122, 124
labour turnover, 12, 66
leader(ship), 5, 6, 11, 91
letters, as method of communi-
    cation, 47, 50, 61
Lewin, Kurt, 3
Likert, Rensis, 111n.
loyalty, 22, 26, 95, 97, 100, 106,
    107, 109, 121, 132

Main Board, 16, 17, 18, 63, 67,
management, author's definition,
    12

management conferences, 58,
    63–8
management development, 21
management-employee relations
    97, 98–9, 100, 101, 106–7,
    116–17
management organization chart,
    53, 60, 61, 137
management research, 143–5
    (App.)
management-staff panels, 111–
    126
advantages for participants
    and their staff, 120–2
first panel meeting, 118, 166–
    171 (App.)
general inferences, 123–6
method, 112–16
post-meeting questionnaire,
    119–23, 164 (App.)
pre-meeting questionnaire,
    116–18, 162 (App.)
management task, the, 22–3
manager, author's definition, 12
managing director, the, 56, 64,
    111, 113, 114, 134, 141
Manchester, University of, 19,
    20, 24n.
Marks & Spencer, 22
Massarik, F., Weschler, I. R.,
    Tannenbaum, R. &, 91
Mayo, E., 8
McGregor, Douglas, 7, 125
meetings, as method of com-
    munication, 51, 58, 75,
    77, 81, 84, 85, 88, 90, 99,
    103, 111, 135, 137, 140
memos, 56
merchanting division, 17, 115
message, type of, conveyed, 59
methods used in author's inquiry,
    23–4

Mills F and G, first study in, 25–41
conclusions, 38–41, 129
daily record for mill manager, 32 (table)
interview checklist, 151–2 (App.)
method of analysis, 31–4
method of investigation, 29–31
monthly summary of daily records for operatives in Mill G, 33 (table)
patterns of information
for mill managers, 32 (table)
for operatives, 34 (table)
for supervisors and specialists, 32 (table)
for three groups of employees, 34 (table)
questionnaires given to
mill managers, 36–7, 150 (App.)
operatives, 38, 148 (App.)
supervisors and specialists, 37, 149 (App.)
results, 34–6
summary statements of, 155–156 (App.)
Mills F and G, follow-up study in, 69–91
assessment of results, 86–9
conclusions, 129–31
management, 89–91
questionnaires given to
operatives, 74–8, 82–6, 156–157 (App.)
supervisors and specialists, 70–4, 78–82, 158–9 (App.)
summary statements of first study, 69–70, 155–6 (App.)
Mill H, study in, 92–110

analysis of questionnaire responses, 96–107
assessment of results, 107–10
management, 96–8
method of investigation, 94–5
operatives, 100–7
questionnaire given to sample of employees, 96–107, 160–1 (App.)
supervisors and specialists, 98–100
Ministry of Labour, 24
Moonman, Eric, 11
morale, 57, 58, 61, 62, 81, 97, 99, 104, 108

newer members of Group, attitudes of, 25, 26, 56,
news bulletin, 60
newsletters, 62, 75
newspapers, 46, 50, 129
news-sheet, 52, 82, 122
notice boards, 41, 81, 84, 85, 88, 102

older members of Group, 25, 56, 90
operatives, *see under* Mills F and G; Mill H
organization chart of Group, 16
organization charts, 53, 60, 61, 137
organization structures, 8–10, 61, 132, 135
organizational change, 46, 49, 51, 63,
organizational difference between firms in stable and in changing situations, 10
organizational responsibilities, 128
organizational theory, 10

panels, *see* management-staff
    panels
Pelej, Joseph, 127 and n.
pensions, 66
personal contact, 61
personalities, 5–6, 46, 63, 127
personnel
    function, 108, 110, 129, 136,
      137
    information, 39, 43, 44, 48,
      49, 50, 81, 82, 85, 90
    management, 97, 99, 104, 128
personnel and training, director
    of, 64–6, 110, 113, 114, 115,
      116, 118
Plessey, 22
printing, 17
productivity, 96–7, 99, 103, 107,
    108, 133
promotion, 96, 98, 99, 102, 107,
    115, 117, 119, 121, 124
psychology in industry, 5, 10
purchasing director, 29

questionnaires, *see under* head
    office; Mills F and G; Mill H

Raphael, Winifred, 141
rapid growth of Group, 21–2
    difficulties attributed to, 52,
      54, 55, 58, 61, 62
recruitment, 14, 21, 28
Report on Wearwell & Co. Ltd/
    University of Manchester
    Project, 21–4
report-writing, 10
research, suggestions for further,
    140–1
Rice, A. K., 8, 10
Roberts, Dr A., 12
Roethlisberger, F. J. & Dickson,
    W. J., 8

roles, 20, 23, 49, 67, 114
rumour, 80, 82, 87
    see also grapevine

Schmidt, W., Tannenbaum R.
    &, 5
Shirley Institute, 24
social contact between personnel,
    13
sociology in industry, 5–7, 10
specialist units
    authority of, 21
    growth of, 22
Sprott, W. J. H., 6, 7
staff panels *see* management-staff
    panels
Stalker, G. M., Burns, T. &, 9
Stockdale, G., 134
structure of Wearwell Group,
    15–18
style, 11
supervisors and specialists, *see*
    under Mills F and G; Mill H

takeovers and policy, 46, 82
Tannenbaum, R., 5, 91
Tavistock Institute of Human
    Relations, 24
technical information, 36, 37, 38,
    39, 40, 43, 44, 48, 49, 50, 73,
    76, 78, 81, 82, 84, 85, 86,
    88, 90
telephone, as method of com-
    munication, 35, 39, 47, 50,
    61
textile depression (1951), 28
textile industry, the, 1–2
training, 53, 62, 84, 88, 93, 115,
    121, 122, 132, 136
Training within Industry meth-
    ods, 66
'training with responsibility', 65

Trist, E. L. & Bamforth, K. W., 10

understanding and appreciation of research work by executives, 19–20, 146–7 (App.)
United Steel Companies Ltd, 138, 139
University of Manchester, 19, 20, 24n.

visits, as method of communication, 47

visits made by author within Group, 20

Weschler, I. R., Massarik, F., Tannenbaum, R. &, 91
Wilson, A. T. M., 20
worker control, 111
worker's understanding of technological change, 12
works managers' meeting, 35, 40, 41, 129
written notices, 41

Yugoslavia, 111